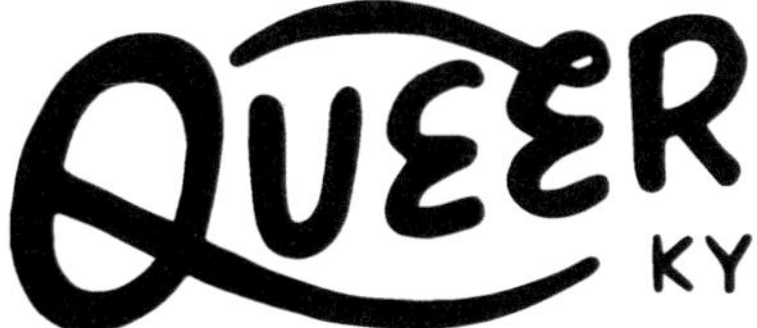

Queer Kentucky is a diverse LGBTQ+ run non-profit based in Kentucky working to bolster and enhance Queer culture and health through storytelling, education, and action. Through our storytelling approach, we give visibility and celebrate the lives of LGBTQ+ people in the great Bluegrass State. Visibility alone is life-saving. Queer Kentucky actively works with organizations and businesses on their inclusivity efforts that enhance the well-being of their employees.

Dedication
To every Queer person struggling, and to all those
that have succumbed to their struggles.
Please know you aren't alone.

And to the thriving LGBTQ+ people and allies
working to enhance the lives of our community.

We see you fighting, and we're standing with you.

DONATE/SUBSCRIBE

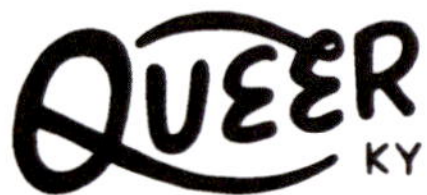

Executive Director
Missy Spears

Editor-in-Chief
Spencer Jenkins

Associate Editor
Hallie Decker

Design
Hannah Schiller,
Brackish Creative

Contributing photographers and artists
Beth Burrows
Ceirra Evans
Faulkner Morgan Archive
Frankie Fiore
Jon Cherry
Matt Pruitt
Michelle Elliott
Milkman Photography
Reed Sampley
Ryan Grant
Samuel Greenhill

Contributing writers
Austyn Gaffney
Belle Townsend
Duncan Cherry
Faulkner Morgan Archive
Kevin Garner
Missy Spears
Nico Lang
Sara Havens
Spencer Jenkins
Spencer Adkins
Tom Lally
Tony Lewis
Will Whaley

Web development
Honeywick

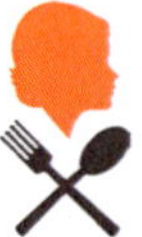

LEE INITIATIVE LUNCH BREAK

For the past two years, Queer Kentucky and
the Lee Initiative have partnered to uplift
Queer voices in the hospitality industry.

For advertising inquiries
contact@Queerkentucky.com

CONTENTS

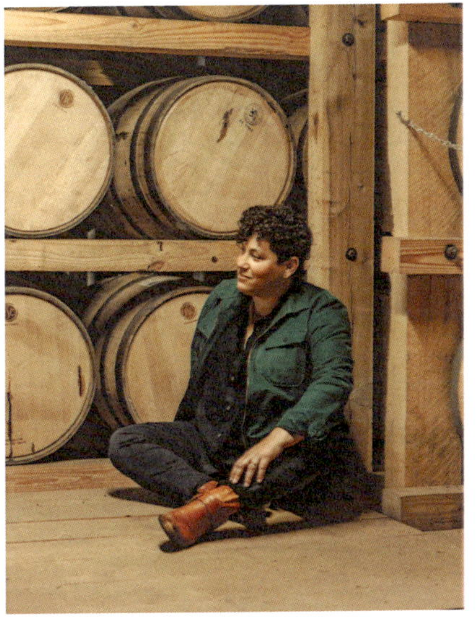

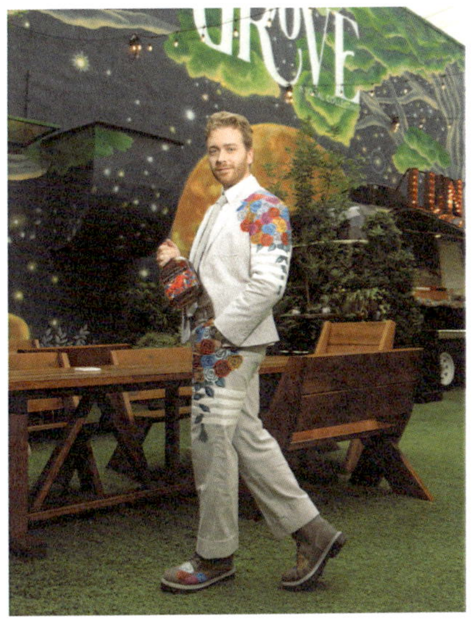

& more

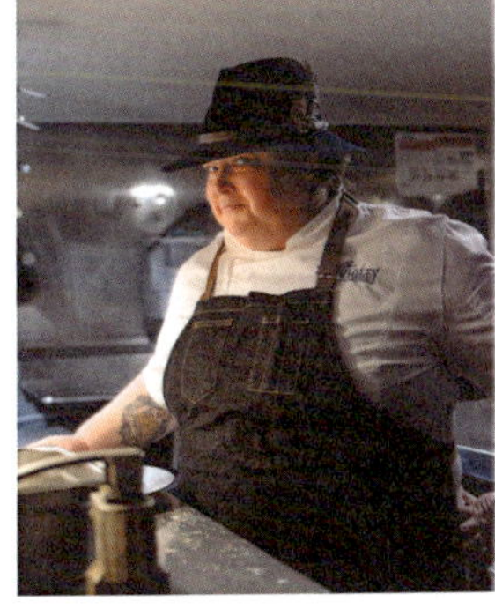

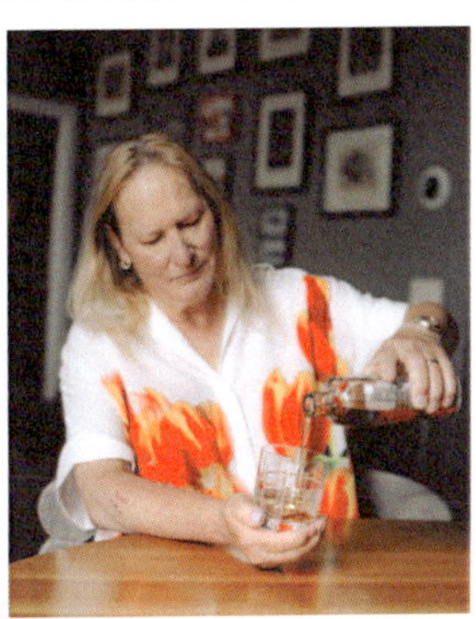

It's happening.

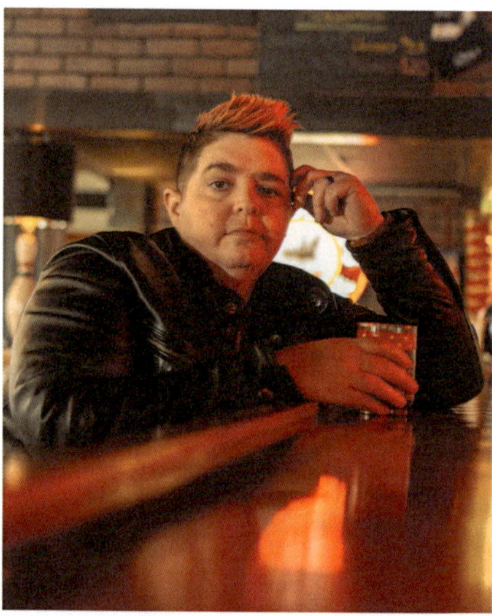

After over a year of working behind the scenes on this project, our team couldn't be more excited to bring you Bourbon and Belonging: Kentucky's Queer Bourbon Week. Over five days and across eight cities in October, participants will partake in dozens of curated experiences across Kentucky including rare tastings and tours, upscale dinners, pool parties, art events, drag brunches, dance parties, and experiences specifically planned for our sober community.

Leading the charge on a statewide bourbon week spanning eight markets isn't within our normal scope of work at Queer Kentucky, but at its core Bourbon and Belonging is about including the LGBTQ+ community in Kentucky's largest industry. We are moving past bourbon's predominantly cis, male, straight, and white image to show that bourbon, as well as Kentucky, is Queer, inclusive, and for all of us. We live in a state, and a country, that works hard to push our community down. This event is us pushing back, hand in hand with the biggest bourbon brands in the world.

Let's face it, the LGBTQ+ community has had a complicated relationship with corporate America over the years. The rainbow profile pictures come down on June 30 as quickly as they go up on June 1, representing that their time of allyship has come to a neatly packaged end for the year. Love it or hate it, we live in a society where freedom and fairness are determined by where the money flows, and our elected officials are far more likely to back off of anti-Queer legislation when AT&T or Toyota speak up, instead of their actual constituents. As conflicted as I have felt at times, I have so much fear for the day that they don't bother to show up at all. And with events like Bourbon and Belonging, I continue building hope for Kentucky.

Kentucky is Bourbon, Kentucky is beautiful, Kentucky is complicated, and Kentucky is Queer.

And this October, I invite all of you to celebrate this with us.

Missy

Dear reader,

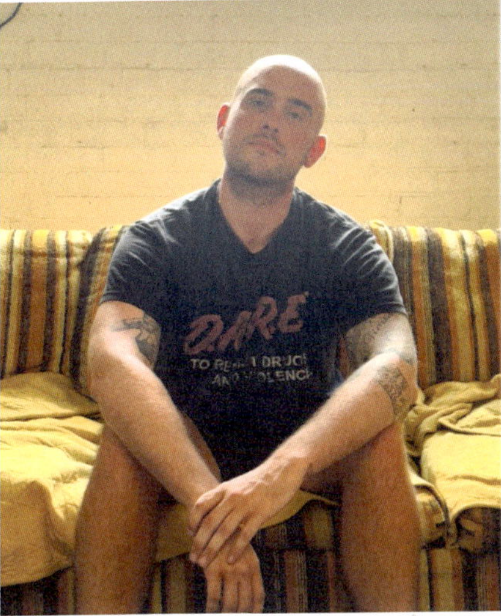

Recently, a few Bourbon tasters and tour guides educated me on the aging process of Kentucky's state sprit, and I couldn't help but notice its parallels with Queer Kentucky. At minimum, Bourbon must age for two years, during which time it develops taste and character through each of Kentucky's distinct seasons. But, it isn't until about six years of maturity that Bourbon begins flourishing in its full flavor and transforms into its true colors. With every "Angel's Share" barrel breath, the more admiration it receives.

Queer Kentucky is six years old. We're sustainably (kind of) funded, staffed with amazing creatives, and aging with grace and sophistication. And wouldn't you know it? Our admiration from Kentuckians and people around the world has grown. Never would I have thought that my little gay blog would eventually spearhead a statewide tourism event like Bourbon and Belonging: Kentucky's Queer Bourbon Week.

Relationships can be complex though, right? As a Bluegrass boy, I love Kentucky. I find home in our rolling hills and miles of splintered black fences. I find ancestral roots in the hollers of Laurel County where my family's story begins. And I find my sense of self through the gritty, glorious and glam-ish streets of my hometown of Louisville.

And though my love for my home is fierce, two things can be true at the same time — I sometimes resent Kentucky. Our state leaders actively harm our Queer community with hateful legislation. Conservative values push many of us deeper and deeper into the darkest closet you'll ever know. Also, I'm allergic to horses — so that sucks.

I have a similarly complex relationship with Kentucky's Bourbon industry: I respect and sometimes resent it.

On one hand, my family collects the beautiful Kentucky Derby editions of Woodford Reserve bottles and proudly displays them along our bar tops and mantles. Hot toddies once soothed my sore throat and stuffy nose, and I have fond memories of Bourbon Festival breakfasts in Bardstown including fluffy Bourbon infused pancakes and butter — an experience not to be missed. And most importantly, during Queer Kentucky's early fermentation years, Bourbon powerhouse Brown-Forman saw the value in our mission and granted us some of our initial funding. Bourbon has offered a lot to my life.

On the other, and as a person in recovery from alcohol and drugs, our relationship is complicated. With the theme of this issue, and the launch of Bourbon & Belonging, I won't lie and say happiness was my only emotion. I was anxious, stemming from the fact that I would be inundated with Bourbon content for months on end, possibly triggering an urge to drink.

As you flip through the pages of ISSUE 06: Queering the Bourbon Industry, you'll find LGBTQ+ industry trailblazers and innovators, Queer stories of hope in recovery, and the love and life Bourbon offers Kentucky. I hope this issue shows the world that Bourbon is diverse, Queer, femme, butch and everything in between.

Love,

THE FOUR HORSEMEN

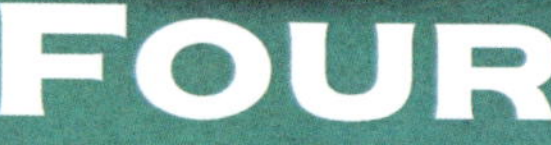
Duncan Cherry *he/him* *@mistersparkle*

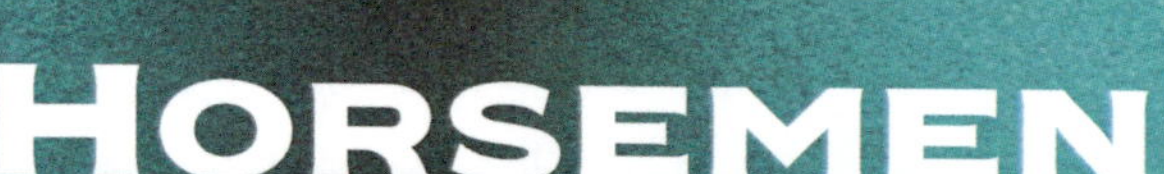
Images by Matt Pruitt *he/him* *@mbpruitt*

As I step into Bar 32 located in Covington, I'm overwhelmed by a sense of nostalgia. The bar instantly feels like home, where the regulars converse like they've known each other for years (which they probably have) and visit this place frequently (which they probably do). It reminds me of the neighborhood bars in Louisville that have the uncanny ability to calm someone as soon as they step inside.

Amy Mobley has owned Bar 32 in Covington for 10 years, though she worked at the bar for years prior when it was formerly a bear bar.

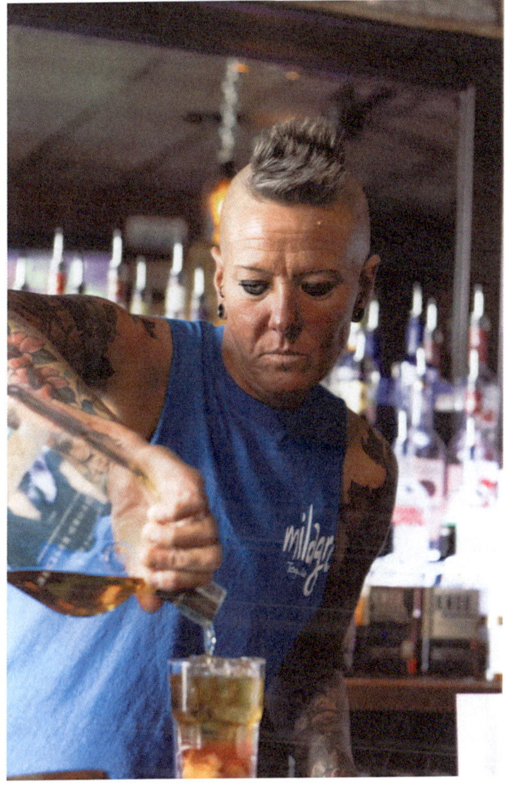

a scoop of ice and mixes the drink to incorporate its citrus and sugar elements with the 90-proof spirit. "It's one of the most iconic Bourbon cocktails there is."

When asked about the importance of Queer spaces, Amy tells me that she always says "we have to keep these kinds of bars open, because there's nothing like walking into a bar and you know you're safe and can be yourself." She smiles, "We have to keep them open, and I am happy to still be here."

Giving back to her community is also vital for her.

"I just want all of the gay people and all of the Queer people to feel welcome," she says, her tattooed skin radiating in the sun from the large windows that make up the bar's front area. "I used to do ladies' night and bear nights, and it felt like it was excluding certain people on those nights. I took all the labels away and made it an everyone bar, and it took off."

She drops some oranges and cherries into a glass behind the bar, adds some bar syrup, and muddles the fruit before a healthy pour of Woodford Reserve finds its way into the cocktail.

"I went with an Old Fashioned because it's one of the first Bourbon drinks I learned to make almost 15-20 years ago. It's nostalgic." She adds

"When I look out, and we have a fundraiser for something, I can see everyone coming together—gay, straight, old, young, trans men, trans women, everybody—and they're having a good time together, that's when I think, 'that's why I do this.' And it's the best feeling, like, oh my god, I created this."

I can tell Amy is always a sight for sore eyes to Bar 32's patrons. A man walks into the bar and sits a few stools away from me. Before I even notice him, Amy approaches, opening a beer and sitting it down in front of him.

"Y'all got any coffee?" he inquires, "I can make a pot if you'd like," Amy replies. "That would be great," the man replies, taking a deep breath and relaxing into the bar's welcoming embrace.

JAKE BRAY

he/him BIG BAR, LOUISVILLE, KY

If you've ever had an exciting Queer night out in Louisville, chances are you've taken a mirror selfie at Big Bar's neon-lit bathroom. And if you did, Jake was probably behind the bar, serving up cocktails and greeting every patron with a warm and welcoming smile. Big Bar is the go-to spot for Queer nightlife in Louisville, from its beginnings as a not-so-big bar to its current multi-level form, offering drinks, dancing, and a delightful atmosphere encompassing all walks of life.

Jake Bray has worked at Big Bar since 2018, where he started his bartending career. Originally from outside Niagara Falls, he went to bartending school in New York State and found his footing in North Carolina before eventually moving to Louisville with his brother. While bar-hopping one night, he met Big Bar owner Kevin Bryan, who offered him a job at the bar the next day. Since then, Jake has become a champion of Louisville's Queer nightlife, as well as an avid music lover, and a model in the River City.

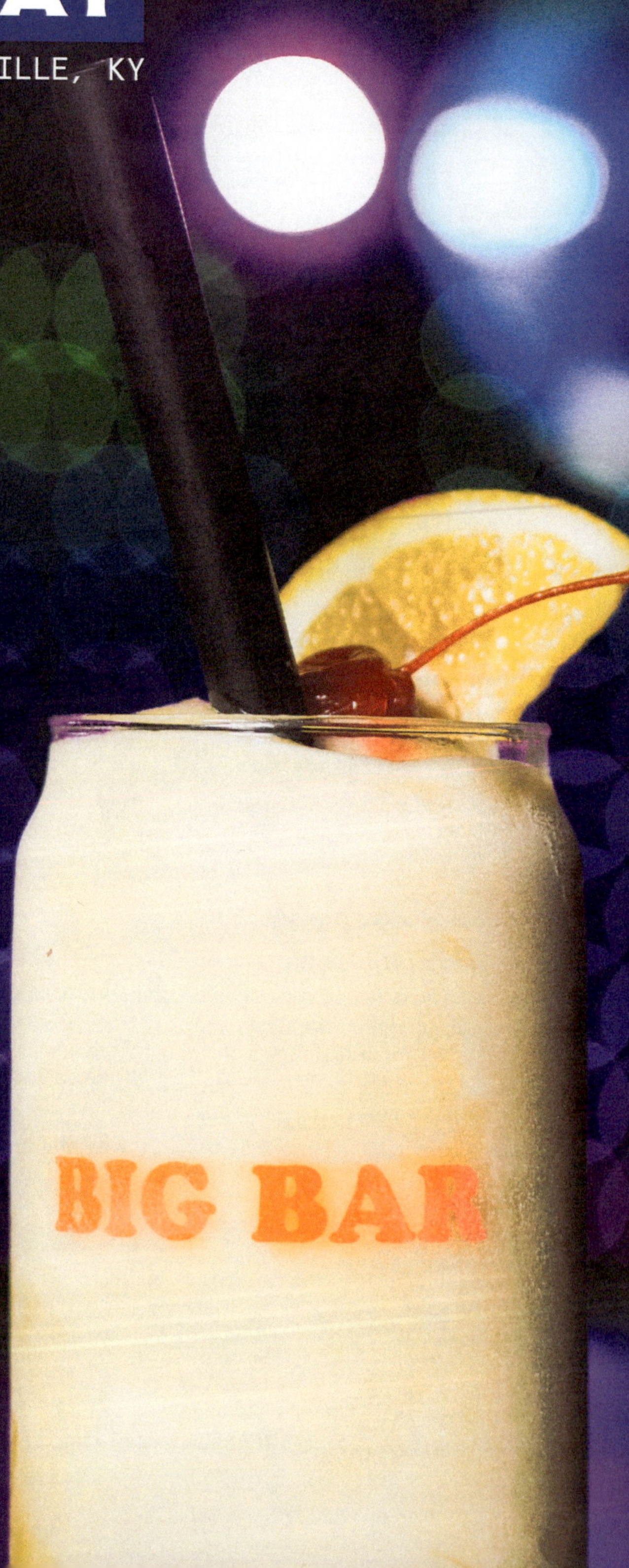

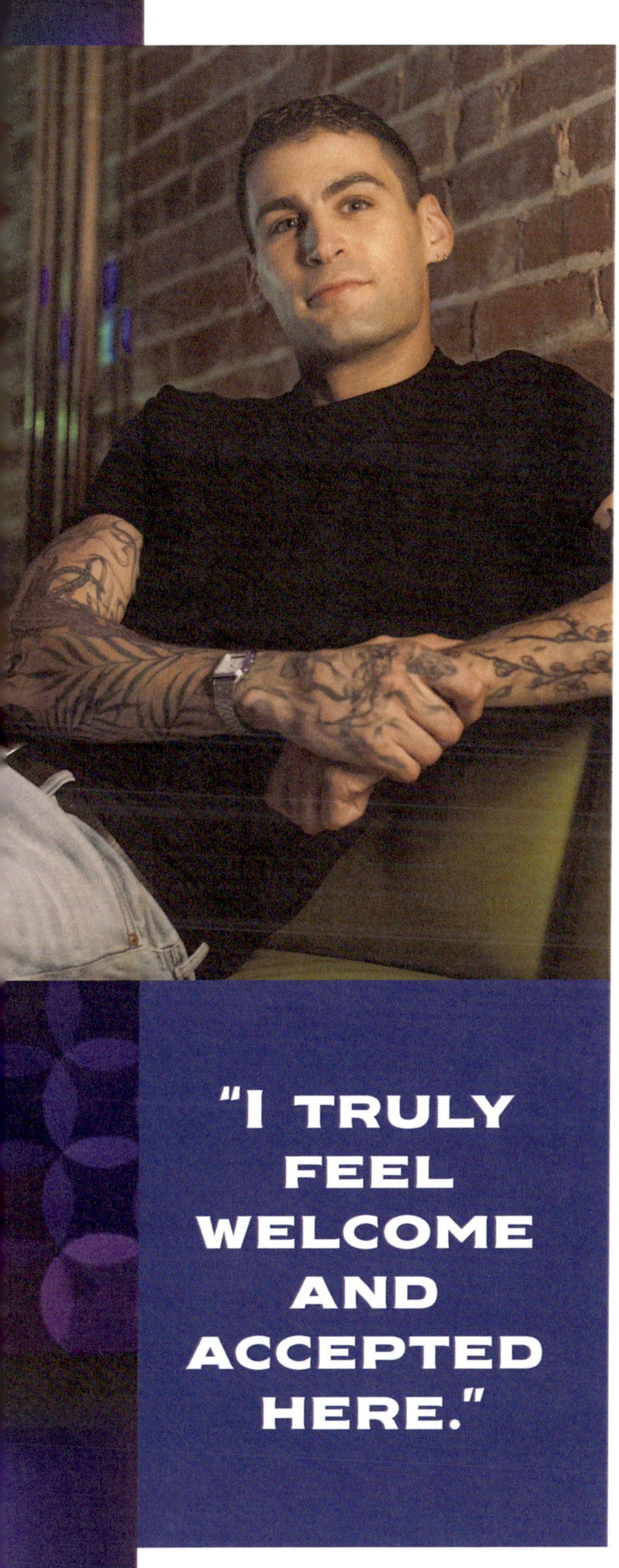

While most gay bars may pour you a vodka-cran or tequila soda, Big Bar has a hidden gem – something more icey. Nestled between their bar and the coolers housing your favorite canned drinks, Big Bar has two rotating flavors of frozen refreshments in their slushy machine.

"Our frozen Bourbon slushy has accents of orange and pineapple juice, lime, and Old Forester Bourbon. So you're getting a full craft cocktail while still being able to cool down. We're a high-volume bar, so this is my favorite drink because it's quick but still carefully curated and perfect for enjoying on our patio." Equal parts fruity, frozen, and boozy, their slushies are a staple amongst patrons, new and old.

Jake sees the importance of Bourbon in Queer culture. He says that "geographically, Bourbon is a staple, and no matter what community you're in, you should be able to enjoy it." He strives to help curate a safe space for all folks in Louisville, as Big Bar hosts a monthly Lesbian Tea Dance event, RuPaul's Drag Race Watch parties, and Sunday Fundays, in addition to regular weekly karaoke and DJs.

He emphasized the importance of people being able to come into the bar and feel welcomed.

"Coming from North Carolina to Kentucky, and them both kind of being in the Bible Belt, I wasn't sure how I would be received, but I truly feel welcome and accepted here," says Bray. Big Bar recently became one of the first bars to have a single barrel pick of Old Forester, where they have bottles labeled with Big Bar's name on the front of them, proving that they are in for the long haul when it comes to keeping the world of Bourbon culture Queer.

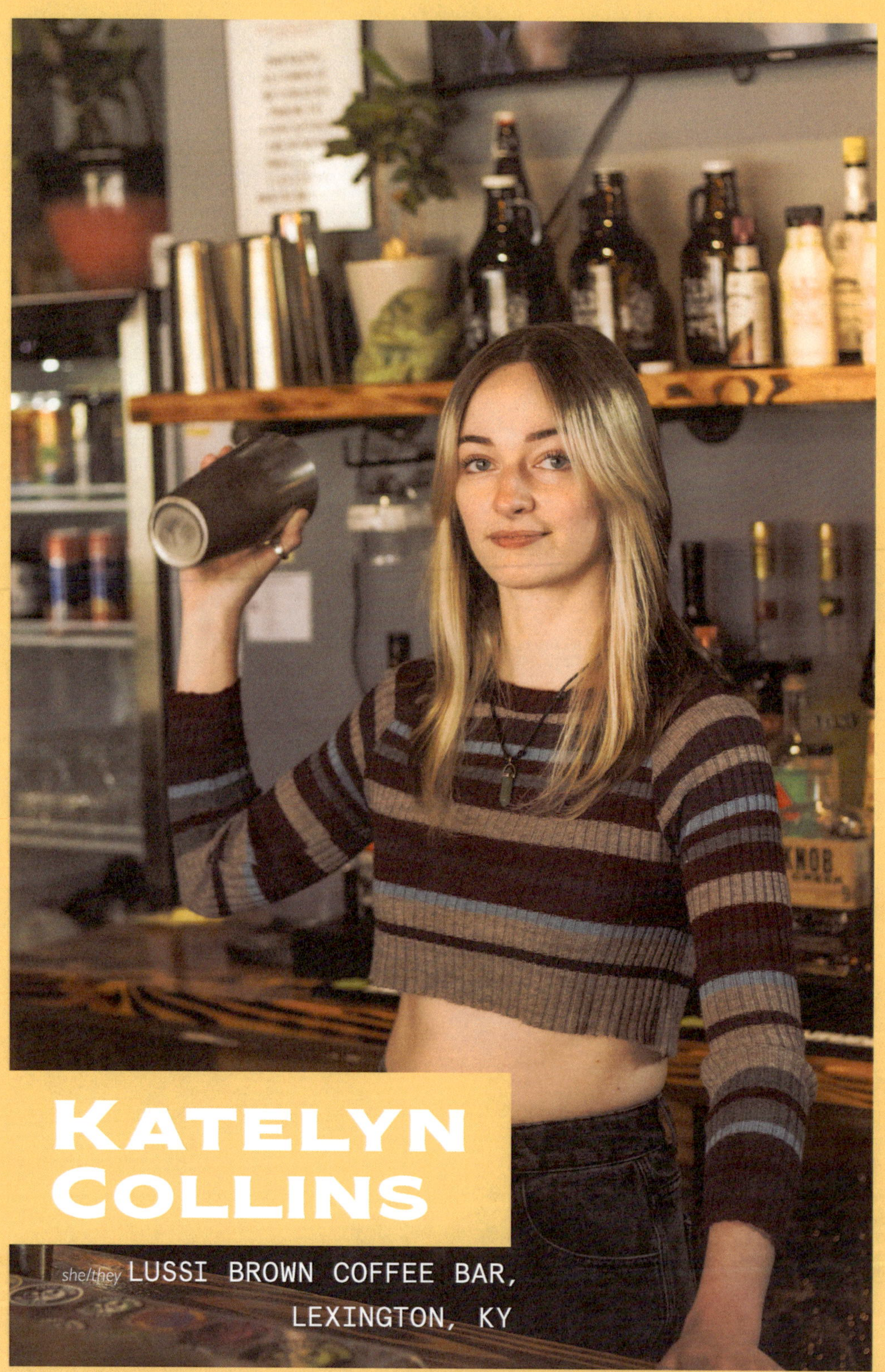

KATELYN
COLLINS
she/they LUSSI BROWN COFFEE BAR,
LEXINGTON, KY

Nestled off Limestone Street, just around the corner from Lexington staple Crossings, you'll find a small but mighty Queer space in Lussi Brown Coffee Bar. This downtown coffee shop and bar proudly showcases its pride through the flags hung above the main window, and the eclectic decor throughout, much of which is sourced from local Queer and trans artists on the wall.

I learned later that Katelyn Collins is the creator of the incredible fiber art butterflies on the wall, as well as a native Kentuckian who has worked at Lussi Brown Coffee Bar for two years.

We talk more at length about getting into the male-dominated Bourbon industry.

"It was interesting to look around at other bars and see men in the industry for 20 years, and it was so intimidating to approach that as a younger Queer woman," she explains.

Collins found a good home behind the bar at Lussi Brown and with co-owner Sarah Brown (half of the bar's namesake alongside co-owner Olivia Lussi), and spoke to the importance of "finding a place like this, where the owners encourage growth and learning and want to help you become better. To be who you are and be proud of who you are, and you find people are going to respect that - especially if you make a damn good drink."

Behind the bar, she stirs up something dark and mysterious - The Cold Fashioned, made with Lussi Brown Cold Brew.

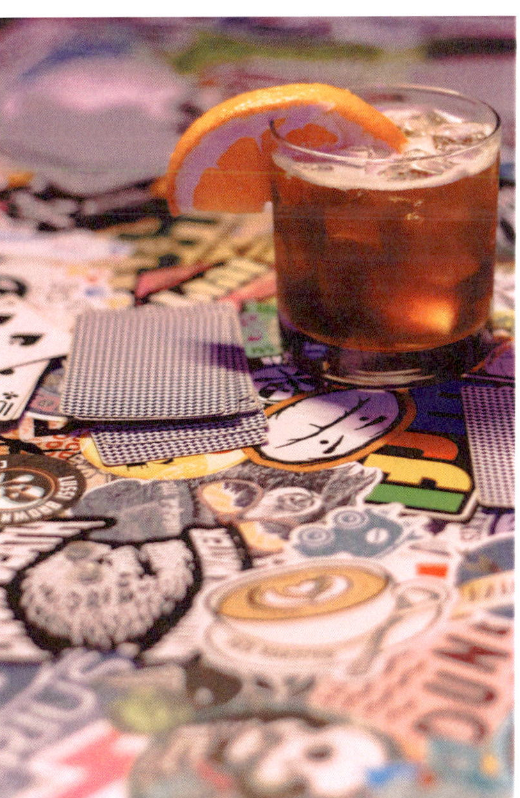

"It's a really nice take on a classic cocktail," Collins says. "Where adding a little bit of the cold brew really accents the citrusy notes of the Four Roses Bourbon, bringing out more of the caramel, that touch of vanilla, and then the cold brew comes back around and rounds it off with the nice bitter touch." They also have the option for Knob Creek Rye, "if you want more of the smoky flavor," as well as a mocktail version for those who choose not to imbibe.

Among the whir of grinding espresso beans up front, we get into where she finds her place in Queer culture, in a setting that is about both nightlife and early mornings.

"I think Queer spaces are important. It's space for us, made by us." She adds, "Those spaces help keep the culture alive and provide that sense of community where people can come and just exist or meet new people; it's a safe space for you to maybe branch into the community if you're just finding your way."

She finishes our conversation by telling me about Lex Lez Night, a sapphic celebration every second Thursday of the month. Lussi Brown hosts pop-ups and mingling from 7 p.m. to 9 p.m., and there's drag, burlesque, and, of course, more drinks (if that's your thing) at Crossings from 9 p.m. until close. "It's honestly such a fulfilling event to work. It's busy, but I have fun during the entire shift. Everyone is so talkative, and you meet so many people."

TAYLOR RENFROE

she/her OLD KENTUCKY BOURBON BAR, COVINGTON, KY

When you visit MainStrasse Village, a national historic district in Covington, you'll find the first ever Bourbon-centric bar in the NKY/Cincinnati area - Old Kentucky Bourbon Bar. Unlike many other Bourbon bars, the vibe of the bar is very relaxed and chill, with walls and shelves lined with over 700 different Bourbons and 200 different American whiskeys.

When you first meet Taylor, she is instantly excited to talk to you; an endless beacon of knowledge about the state's spirit and the place she pours it.

"I was one of the original employees," she tells me in a cozy corner booth inside the bar. "We set out with a goal to be the most welcoming and deliberately inclusive places we could be," and I think they've fully succeeded.

As we explore the wooden-fenced patio, I see several gentlemen enjoying cigars and a couple enjoying a nice pour from the bar's vast selection. Back inside, people of all ages are talking with a friendly bartender about what flavor profile they look for in a Bourbon, carefully aiding them in picking the perfect one.

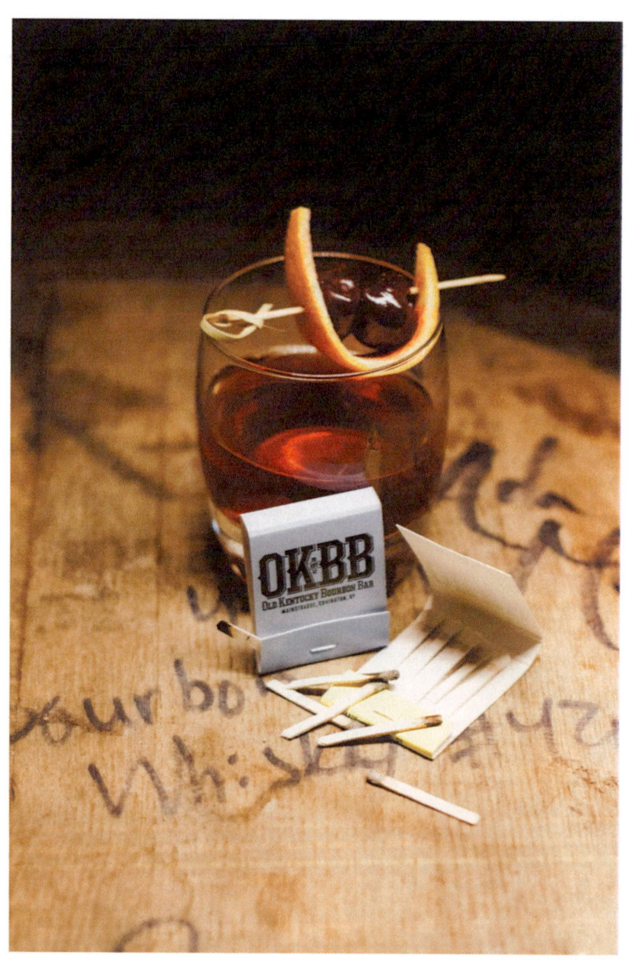

Taylor pulls a few bottles out from behind the bar to begin making a spin on a Vieux Carré. "This is a classic New Orleans drink created in 1920, which traditionally is equal parts rye and cognac with vermouth and Bénédictine. I like using a High Rye Bourbon because it adds warmth and makes for an excellent nightcap."

Though you can tell it's a spirit-forward drink, it's smooth and flavorful, without any burn, even at its high proof. "We use Wild Turkey 101; we are Wild Turkey sluts here. I feel like they get a bit of a bad rap, but it's one of the best whiskeys."

She talks to me a little about being Queer in the Bourbon industry and the importance of having spaces where Queer people feel welcome. "When it comes to a Bourbon bar, there's a stigma that it is not a very inclusive place, it's not very Queer-friendly, not

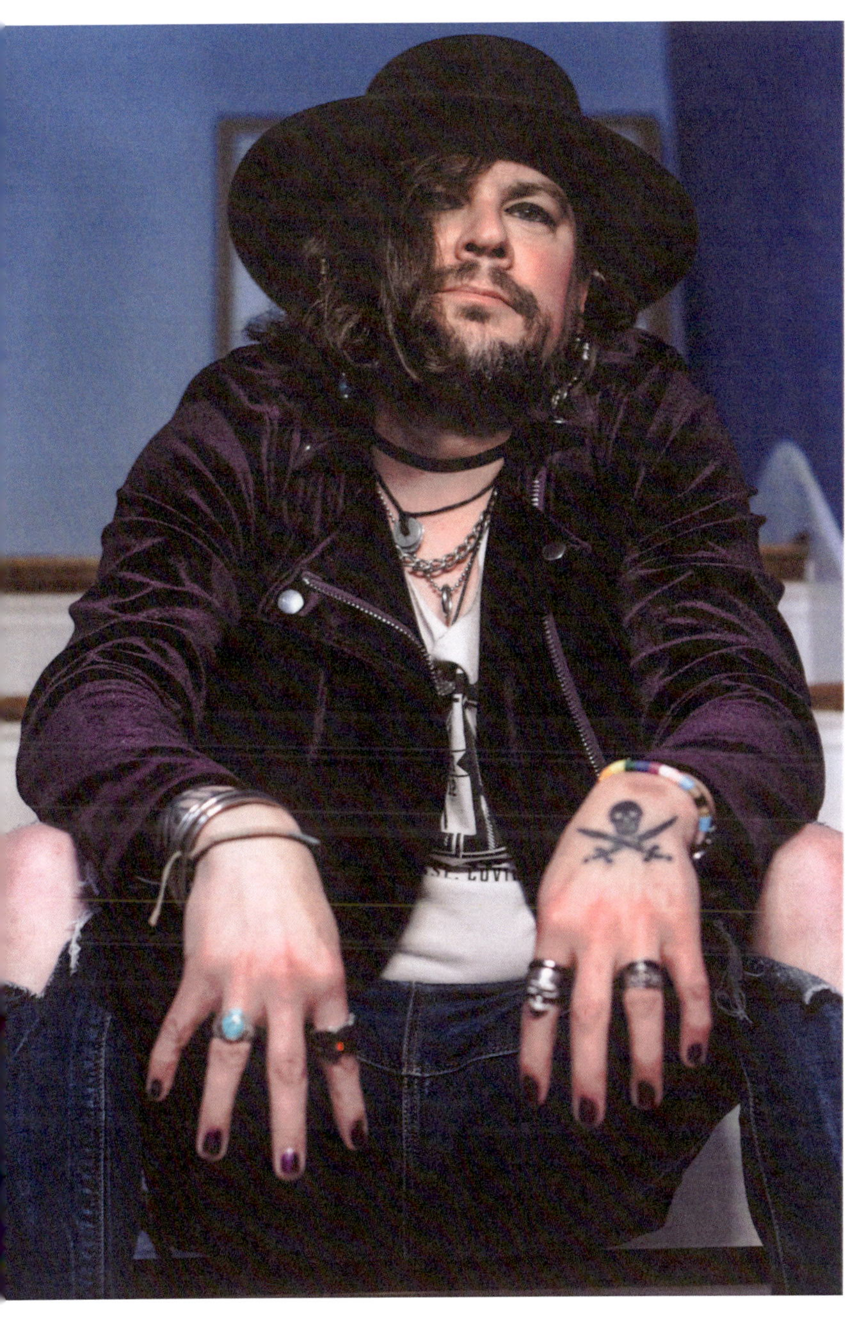

POC friendly, and that shouldn't be the thing and definitely not who we (OKBB) have ever tried to be. [We strive to] create a space with a neighborhood Bourbon bar where you can feel at home."

Taylor adds that working in the industry has helped her find her identity as gender fluid. "It took me quite a while to present the way that I do; a large part of it was just, fuck it, what else are you gonna do?" The support and encouragement of friends helped make that much easier. "You only get one time around, and coming out has been the best time of my life. You're going to encounter some assholes, but you're going to do that anyway, regardless of who you are."

"YOU ONLY GET ONE TIME AROUND, AND COMING OUT HAS BEEN THE BEST TIME OF MY LIFE."

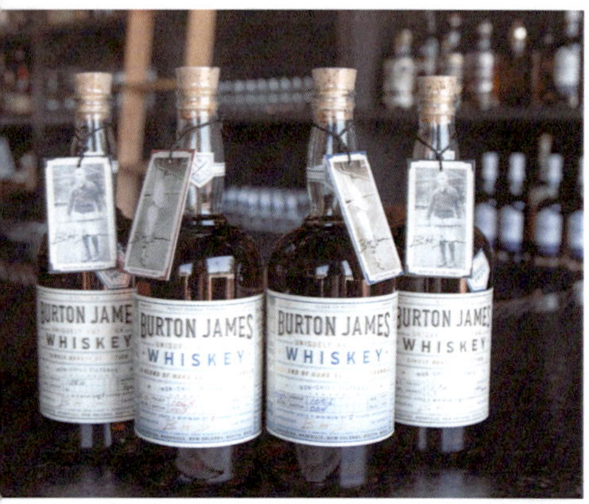

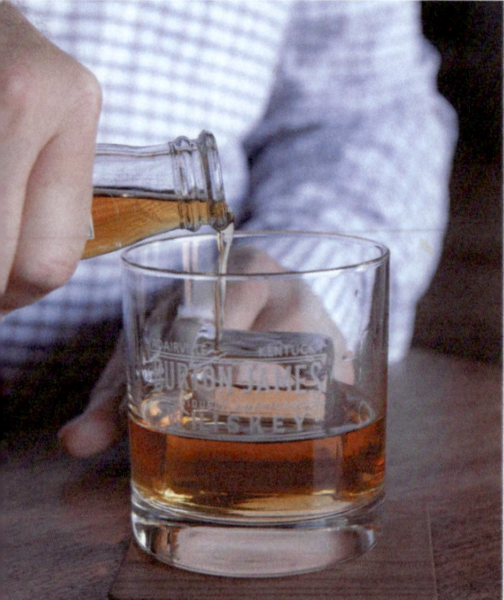

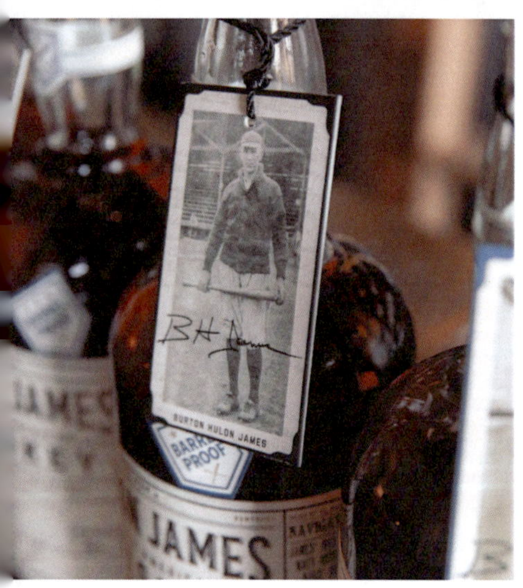

BIG DREAMS IN A SMALL TOWN: BURTON JAMES WHISKEY PUTS ADAIRVILLE ON THE MAP

Sara Havens *she/her @barbelle_lou*

Adairville is a small Kentucky town located in Logan County, about a mile and a half from the Tennessee border. About 800 folks call this farming community home, and most families have resided there for generations. Shawn McCormick is one such resident, and while he wasn't born in Adairville, his family's roots have been firmly planted in the lush soil since the early 1900s.

McCormick, 55, would spend his childhood summers and holidays at his great-grandparents' farmhouse, and he always had a soft spot for small-town life. He returned often throughout his adulthood to visit family, and when the idea to start his own Bourbon distillery struck him in 2012, just as the Bourbon boom was beginning, McCormick only had eyes for Adairville.

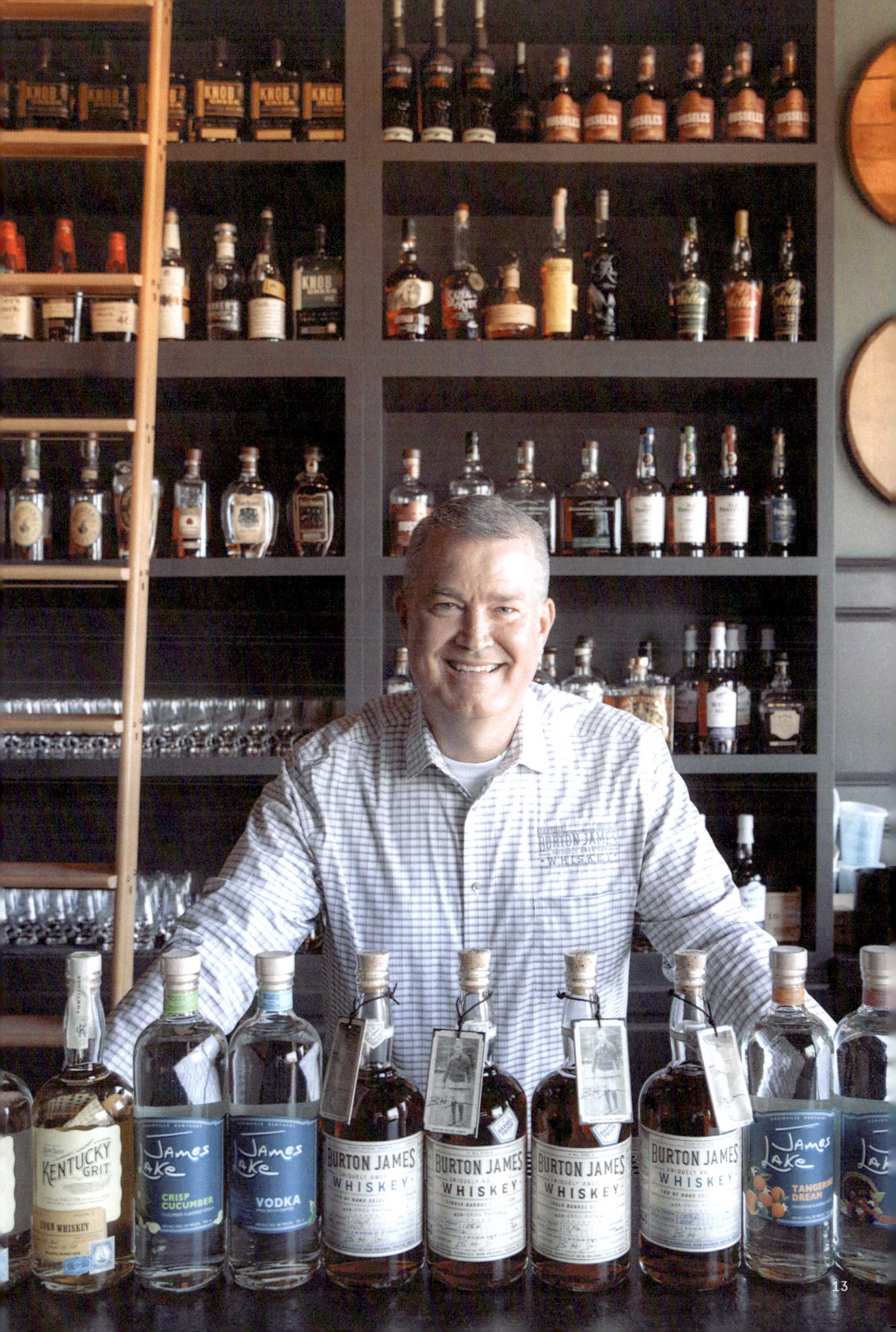

KENTUCKY GRIT
CORN WHISKEY
James Lake
CRISP CUCUMBER
James Lake
VODKA
BURTON JAMES
UNIQUELY AN
WHISKEY
BURTON JAMES
UNIQUELY AN
WHISKEY
BURTON JAMES
UNIQUELY AN
WHISKEY
BURTON JAMES
UNIQUELY AN
WHISKEY
James Lake
TANGERINE DREAM
James Lake

Of course there were many obstacles to face, including the fact that the town was dry, but with patience and persistence, he opened B.H. James Distillers in 2022 in the former Adairville Fire Department on West Gallatin Street, adjacent to the town square. (The residents of Adairville voted to allow alcohol sales in 2017).

B.H. James Distillers is named after McCormick's great-grandfather Burton James, who played professional baseball from 1908-1919. Burton was from Coopertown, Tenn., just across the state line from Logan County, and he met his wife Estelle, from Adairville, at a general store.

After his baseball career, Burton and Estelle decided to make Adairville home, and they purchased Estelle's family farm. McCormick wanted to honor his great-grandfather's legacy with his company. He's currently producing Burton James Whiskey; Kentucky Grit, a corn whiskey, and a line of flavored vodkas under the name James Lake Spirits.

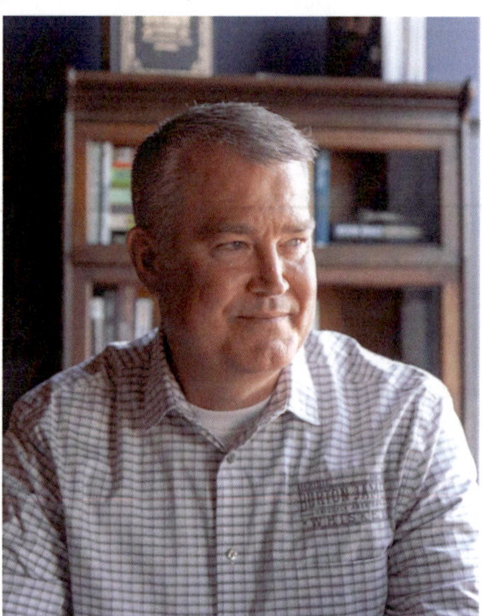

Back when McCormick decided to dip his toe into the Bourbon pool — after visiting a few distilleries on the Kentucky Bourbon Trail in 2012 — he had the foresight to start buying barrels of Bourbon so he would have a supply when the time came to open his own place. So his flagship whiskey, Burton James, is 6-7 years old and packs quite a punch. He's also distilling his own whiskey on a 25-gallon pot still, and he plans to release his first Bourbon on B.H. James' third anniversary in November of 2025.

"What is ironic is when we bottled the first Burton James Whiskey, it was 10 years to the very week I was on the Bourbon Trail," says McCormick, who spent most of his career in product development in the food industry. His goal was to have his own business, and locating it in Adairville is the cherry on top. Every other week, McCormick hosts "Slushie Saturdays" at the distillery, and residents gather to sip some cocktails, play cornhole and enjoy being social.

"My focus now is on community building and making it a place where people can come hang out, meet their neighbors, and have a fun time," he says. "Last year when we were doing cornhole for the first time, I had someone say, 'I've lived here for X-number of years and I never met my neighbor, but I finally met him here.' There's really no socialization in town other than at churches. So if you're not a churchgoer, you're not really meeting your neighbors. There are no bars or restaurants in town, so it's a little tricky meeting people."

McCormick identifies as gay, but it's not something he broadcasts in his new endeavor.

"Since I'm in small-town Kentucky, I'm not overly involved in the Queer life here. But I like to joke, I'm not the only gay in the village," he says. "I'd love to have more of a connection with the Kentucky LGBTQ community. I'm a member, but I guess I'm not out and proud at the moment. All my employees know and most of my family. At the end of the day, I'm just me. No matter what situation I'm in, I'm always just me."

Looking ahead, McCormick would like to expand his operation with a larger pot he still has in storage, and also add a 25-seat bar and lounge area. He wants to offer fun distillery tours and experiences and also join the Kentucky Bourbon Trail. But for now, he wants his whiskey to do the talking, so his focus is to get Burton James on bar shelves throughout Kentucky, putting Adairville on the Bourbon map, and hopefully garnering fans near and far.

YOU BELONG HERE.

Inclusive coworking and community, starting at $299/month.

Story

828 E Market St., Louisville, KY

storylouisville.com

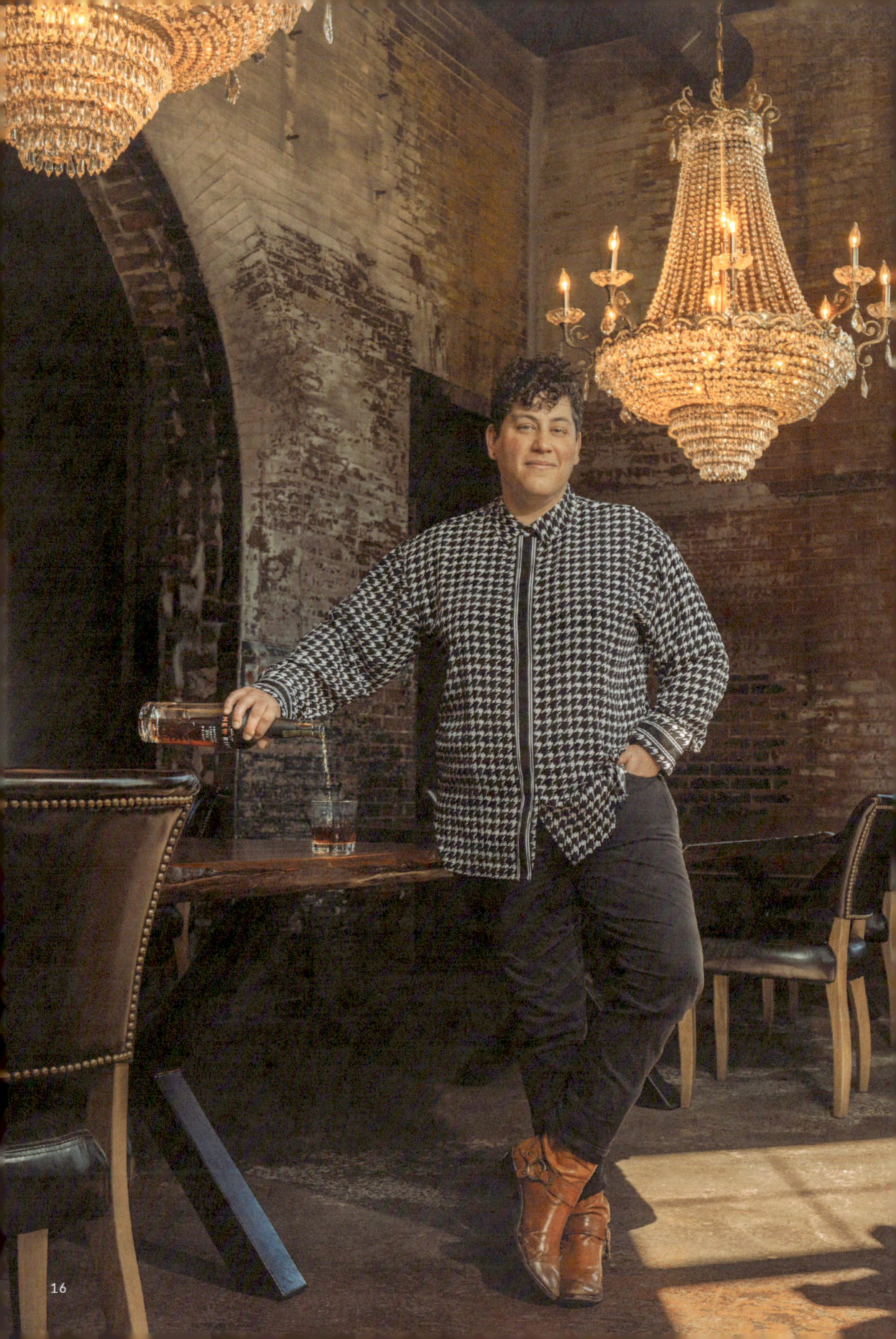

from DOUBT *to* DEVOTION

HOW HANNAH LOWEN REDISCOVERED KENTUCKY'S BOURBON HEART

Missy Spears
she/they   @missy_spears

AFTER SWEARING THAT SHE WOULD NEVER RETURN TO KENTUCKY, IT WAS A HANDSHAKE IN A DOG PARK THAT BROUGHT HANNAH LOWEN BACK.

Lowen was born and raised in Louisville, Kentucky, surrounded by horses, Bourbon culture, and friends who didn't look like her. Both of her parents were New Yorkers who had relocated to Kentucky in the 1970s.

As a child, I did not feel connected to Kentucky because I was so different than my friends and my neighbors because we were Jewish, we had dark curly hair" she explains. "All of my girl-friends from high school are like these beautiful blonde, you know, brilliant women, but I didn't look like them."

Beyond the physical differences were the cultural. Lowen's family didn't go to church. And as she grew up, her interests strayed from the horses, Bourbon, and all things Bluegrass that make up so many Kentucky events. When she graduated from high school she remembers telling people that she would never be moving back to Kentucky. She didn't connect to the heritage…or the humidity.

However, Lowen would backtrack on that vow because the longer she was gone, the more she discovered her love for it. First in Wisconsin, then in Oregon, and later while traveling across Europe. With every new place she visited she couldn't help but compare it to home, and she started constantly surprising herself that Louisville held its own. The foodie scene. The beauty. The Derby. The people and places that made Louisville as unique as any of the cities she spent time in.

In addition to a new appreciation for Kentucky's culture, Lowen was also becoming a fierce supporter of the Bluegrass state. Too many misconceptions about her home, and the people she loved in it, led Lowen to start identifying as a Kentuckian.

They always expected that we were rednecks," she said. "And we were dumb and hillbillies. I mean, my college roommate asked if I wear shoes…for real. That was in the 2000s.

AND SO I THINK IN THAT

I STARTED TO BE LIKE, 'NO, KENTUCKY'S AWESOME.'"

It was also during this time that she first felt connected to an industry. From the micro-breweries in Madison to the craft IPAs in her Portlandia days to the historic variety of beer across Europe, Lowen was growing to appreciate the smells, recipes, and innovation found in craft brewing. Thinking about what she was consuming, how it was made, and who made it was a gateway for her. Lowen loved that she could walk into a brewery off of the street, see the tanks, smell the ingredients, learn about their process, and taste the final product, a rare glimpse into how each variety is made.

And that gateway brings us to a dog park in Louisville, where Lowen met with an old family friend Ken Lewis, owner of The Party Source in Newport, Kentucky, the largest adult beverage superstore in the country.

During their conversation, Ken informed Lowen that he was selling The Party Source to his employees and that he and his daughter were opening a distillery in the same parking lot. Lewis further explained that he wanted Lowen on board.

In that dog park thirteen years ago, they shook on a deal that would see Lowen returning to Kentucky the following year, the one place she was certain she would never live again, to help create "New Riff," the largest distillery in Northern Kentucky.

Since that handshake, New Riff has grown to be one of the most beloved distilleries in the country by not just winning awards for quality, but by living by their mantra of working to lift up their tiny corner of the world.

They have donated hundreds of thousands of dollars to local causes, including over $140,000 during Covid that was distributed to local bartenders and servers who were impacted by the pandemic. They use their space to host community events such as this spring's Queer Soup Night fundraiser. Each June they are a constant presence in the NKY Pride Parade while ignoring the larger Pride PR opportunities on the other side of the river.

"I think that creates a certain openness that you get to be like a reflection of your community. And I think for New Riff for a long time, it was just being a reflection of our team. We weren't doing pride when it was in a parking lot that was flooded because we were trying to make a formal impression, it's because there were Queer people here."

And in her personal life, Lowen has fallen back in love with Kentucky.

"People sleep on Northern Kentucky all the time," Lowen laments. "When we moved here, and I have to give tons of credit to Julia, she was like we need to live in Covington. And then we fell in love with it. There's so much good food, drink, culture, people. It's just in this tiny little place in the world. So there's like great pride in kind of like finding this gem because we're not from here."

"I THINK THE COMMUNITY IS STRONGER. THEY FIGHT ABOVE THEIR WEIGHT."

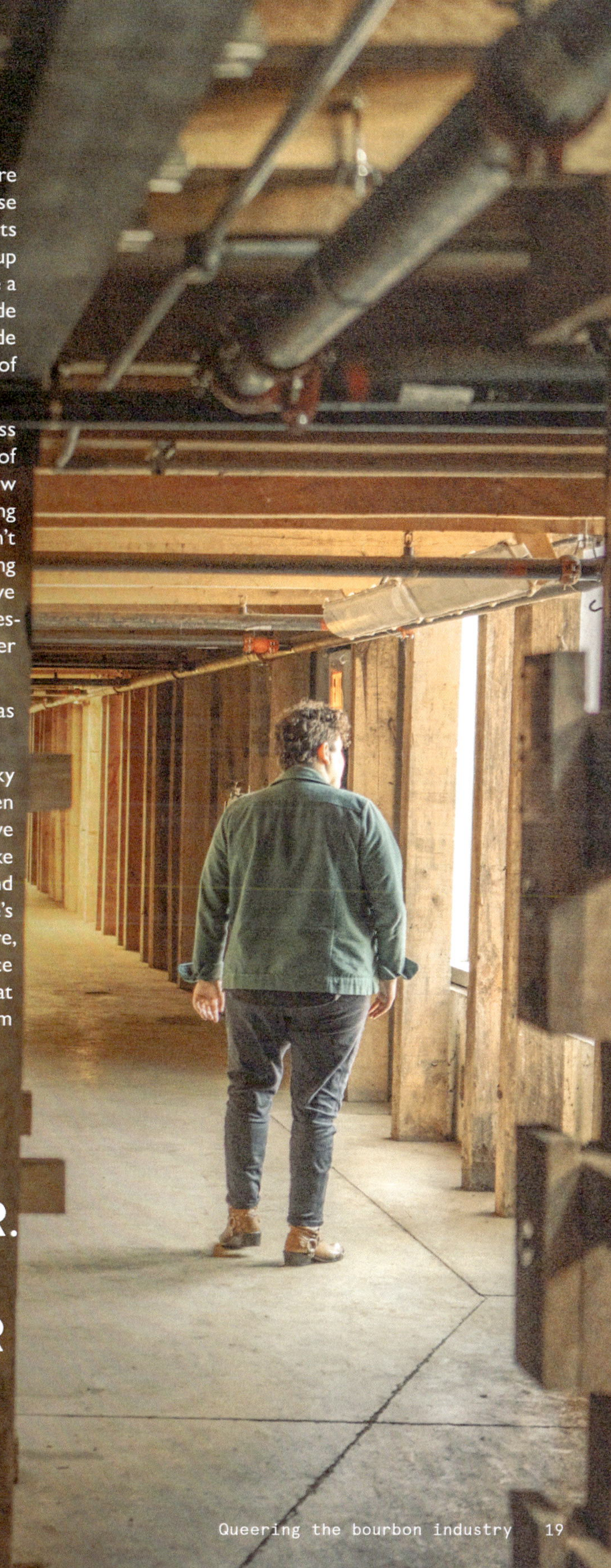

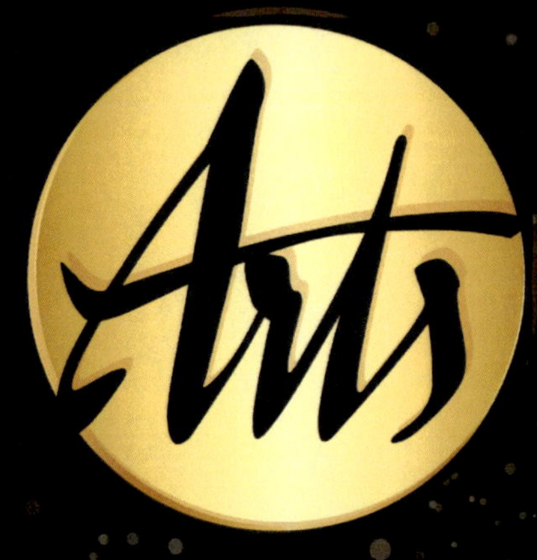

Arts

75 YEARS

IN THE

CITY OF

ARTISTS

CELEBRATE WITH US AT

FUNDFORTHEARTS.ORG

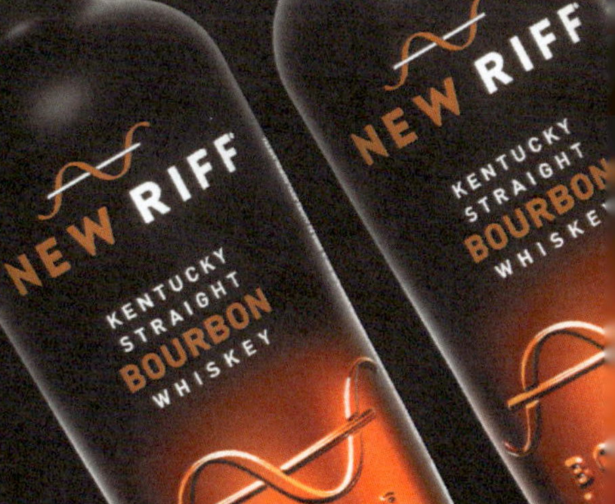

NEW RIFF®
DISTILLING

A NEW RIFF ON AN OLD TRADITION

NEWRIFFDISTILLING.COM | NEWPORT, KY

ETERNITY ✦ WELLNESS

- IV HYDRATION TREATMENTS
- VITAMIN INJECTIONS
- INFRARED SAUNA
- BOTOX & FILLER
- HYDRAFACIAL & CRYOFACIAL
- WELLNESS MEMBERSHIPS
- SCAN FOR FULL MENU!

502.444.8100

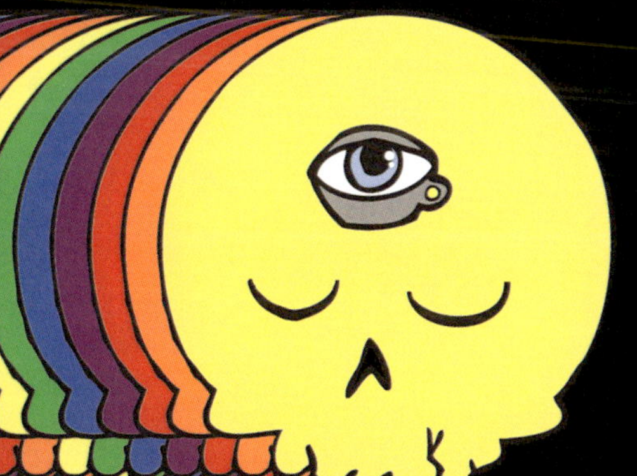

LUSSI BROWN
COFFEE BAR

EST. 2017

LUSSIBROWNCOFFEE.COM

YOUR LOCAL HUB FOR LGBTQIA SUPPORT AND COMMUNITY RESOURCES

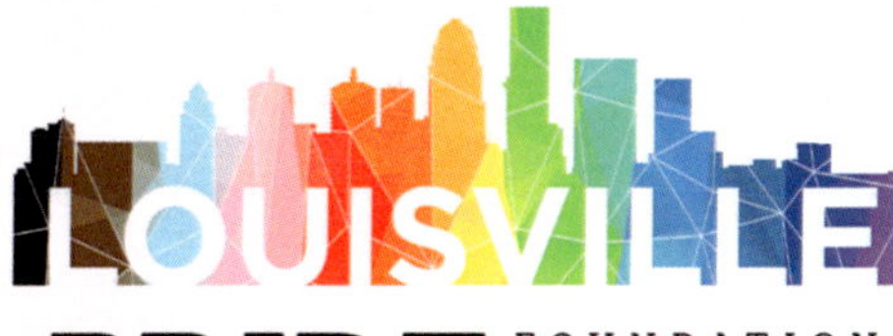

MEETING SPACES

SOCIAL EVENTS

LEARNING PROGRAMS

HARM REDUCTION KITS

AND MUCH MORE!

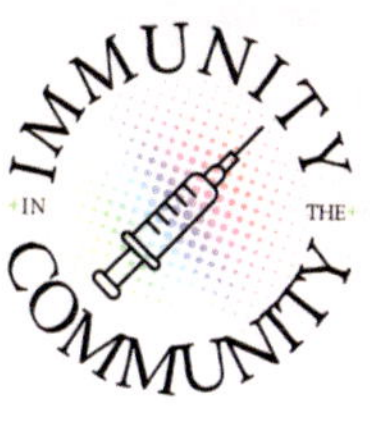

VACCINE CLINICS COMING SOON

1244 S. THIRD STREET LOUISVILLE, KY 40203 | 502-498-4298 | INFO@LOUPRIDEKY.ORG

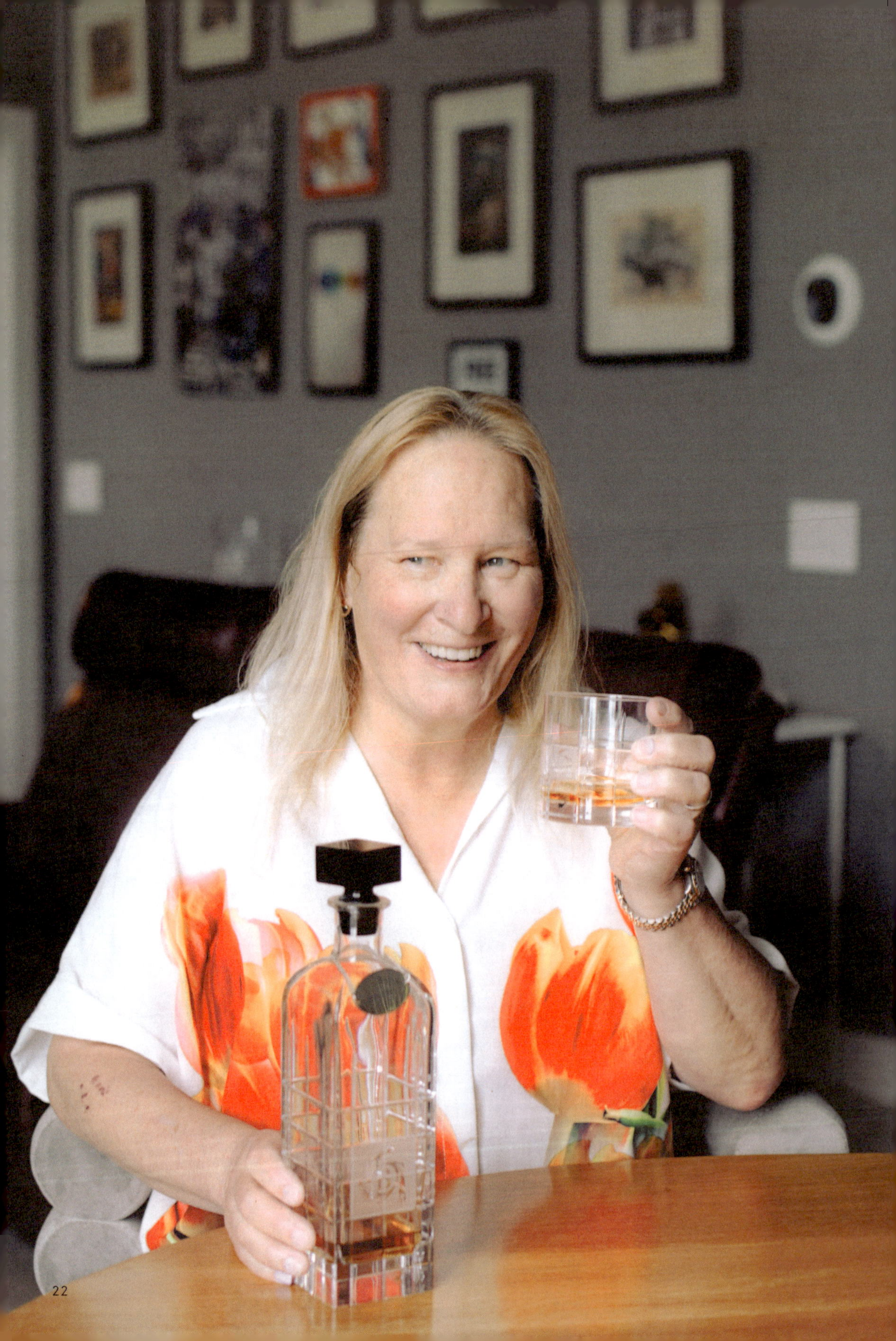

It's Never Too Late to Come Out. Erica Fields is Living Proof.

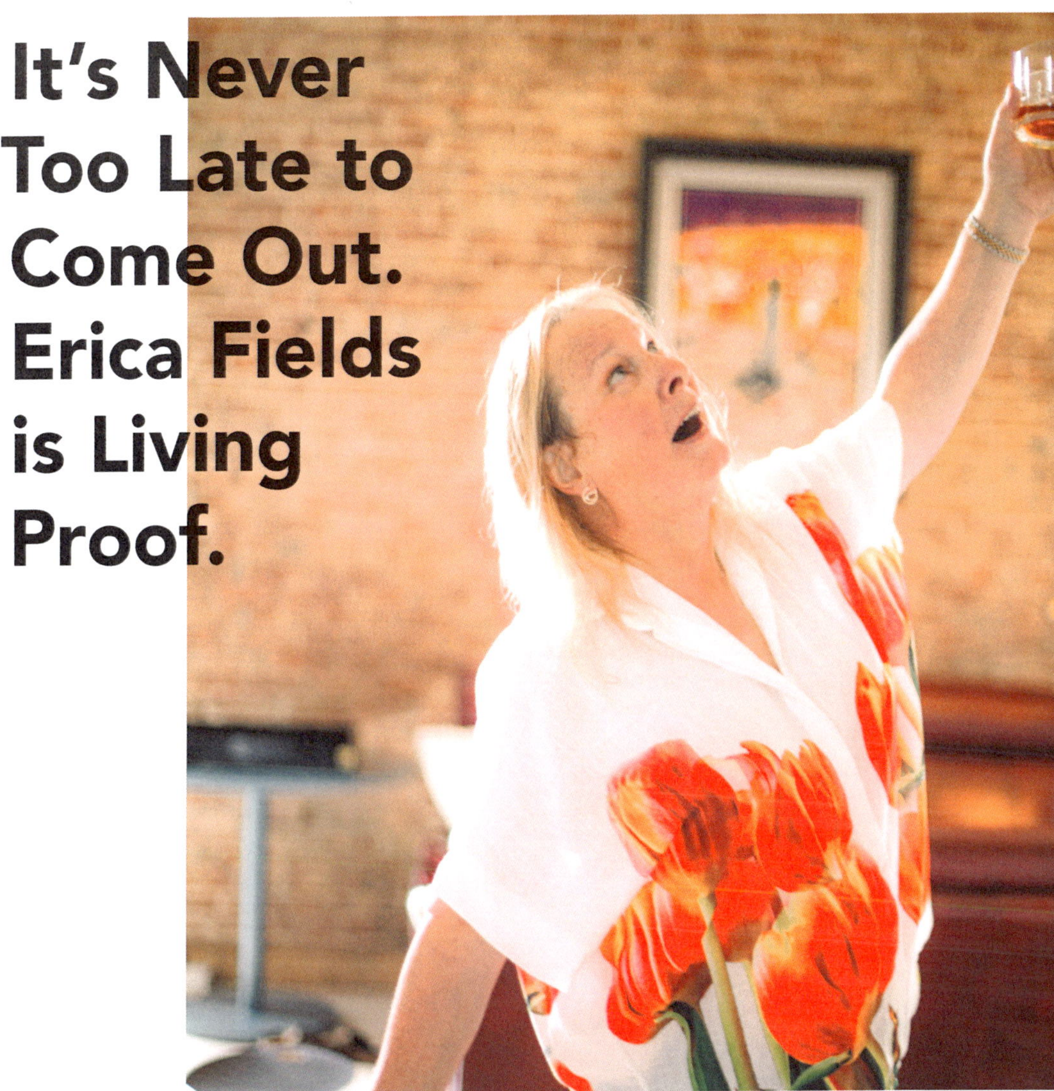

Nico Lang *he/they @Queernewsdaily*

Erica Fields thought she would lose everything if she came out as transgender, so for many years, she didn't. Fields, who is now 70, has been working in the grain industry since 1974, following in her father's footsteps after a brief flirtation with medical school and the theater. What she liked about grain, she says, was participating in history. As a grain trader who worked directly with farmers, Fields felt connected to the earliest Stone Age days of domesticating crops, which later developed into modern agriculture and transport. And Fields loved Bourbon, ever since she and her high school friends snuck drinks in her father's cellar, mixing in water to disguise what they'd imbibed. As she developed a taste for it, she admired the smoothness of Bourbon, the subtle nuances between distilleries, and the way the barrel imparts its own unique flavor into the brew.

Afraid of losing her career and the life she had built for herself, Fields spent years hiding. In her childhood and early adulthood, the androgyne style of the 1960s counterculture movement, where men wore their hair long and favored flowing bohemian shirts with bell bottoms, allowed her femininity to evade notice. But as she grew older, Fields would save gender nonconformity for business trips, wearing women's undergarments under her everyday clothes.

"Anytime you ever heard of or saw someone who was trans depicted in [the media], it was incredibly negative," Fields tells Queer Kentucky. "It was always as a freak. When I was a kid, I would go to the state fair, and I would go to the side show. That's how I felt I would be perceived by everybody. I was a person who really loved human relationships, and I had a lot of them. I believed that I would lose them all, and that scared the shit out of me. I had been living with this secret inside of me since I was around 10 or 12 years old, and I got used to it."

Nearly two decades ago, Fields' secret came to light after her ex-wife discovered some of her feminine clothing while Fields was on a business trip to Winnipeg. Thinking that Fields was having an affair, her ex wanted to know who the garments belonged to. "They're not mine, and they're not my daughter's," she said in a tense phone conversation. "Whose are they?" After a pause, Fields blurted out the truth of what she'd been afraid to acknowledge her entire life. "They're mine," she responded. But instead of feeling as if she had just ruined her entire life, Fields was suddenly gripped by an unexpected sensation: an overwhelming wave of relief. She wanted to go out into the world and "finally find out who I really was," Fields recalls.

Although her marriage ultimately ended, none of Fields' darkest fears came to pass. Her children were accepting, and she grew closer with her oldest sister when there was no longer this unspoken barrier between them. She felt she could be more honest with those around her and more herself. That was true of her work life as well. After reaching out to the National Center for Trans Equality for resources and information, she gave a presentation to her business partners on what it meant to be transgender and why it wouldn't be a problem for their company. She wrote letters to every single one of her colleagues and customers reintroducing herself as Erica, and no one had an issue with it, she says, aside from a "few people out in the hinterlands of the Dakotas."

Fields continued to thrive in an industry where there is little out trans representation, moving from Minneapolis to Lexington in 2017 to take advantage of Kentucky's thriving Bourbon industry. She founded her own grain

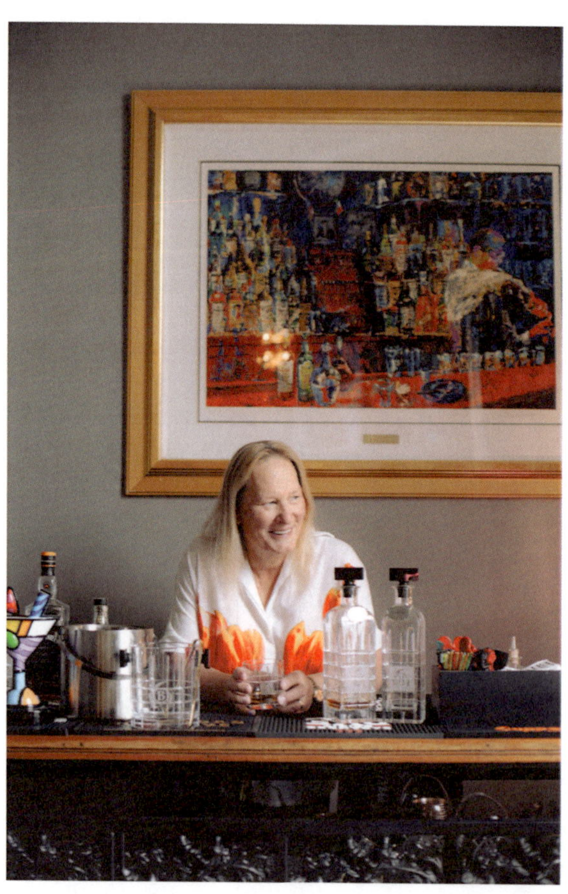

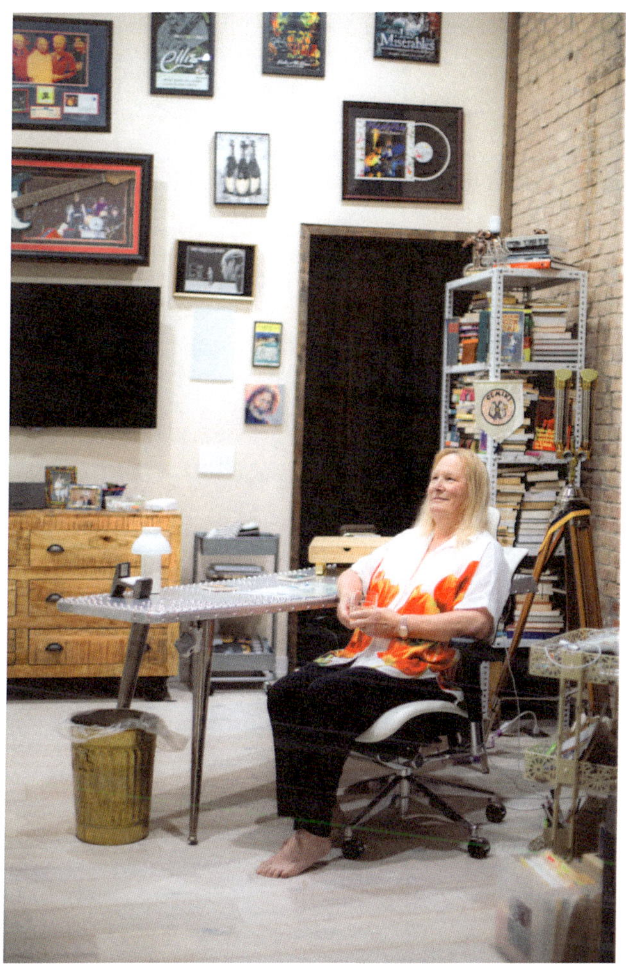

Looking back, Fields' only regret is that she didn't begin her journey sooner. She used to feel such envy watching the other girls at her Catholic school sitting together at lunch in their uniforms and plaid skirts, and when she began transitioning, she worried about being what she calls a "blue hair." "When I was growing up, most old ladies would use hair coloring to cover their gray and it turned blue," she says. "I'm an old lady. I didn't get a chance to be a teenager, I didn't get a chance to be in my 20s, I didn't get a chance to do a lot of the things that I would have absolutely loved to do."

But despite her late start, Fields says that she is so happy to have finally found herself at long last. "When I walk down the street, I don't have a sense of being trans," she says. "I have a sense of being Erica. I know I'm a woman. I walk into a store, and I don't even think about it. My favorite thing about being trans is knowing that I can be who I am."

marketing business, Brooks Grain, LLC, although she is now semi-retired after handing over operations to her nephew. Not one to allow herself to stay idle for long, Fields hopes to start a whiskey company with her new wife, whom she met at a drag cabaret shortly after her divorce. Ultimately, Fields didn't lose anything: She has continued to travel the world and make a significant impact on her community. She was one of the co-founders of CIVITAS, Louisville's LGBTQ+ chamber of commerce; serves on the board of Fund for the Arts, which invests in Kentucky arts organizations; and recently delivered a keynote address at a local K-12 school.

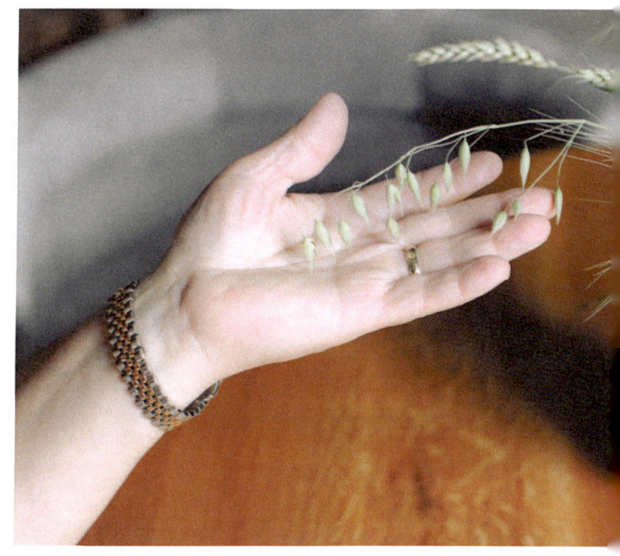

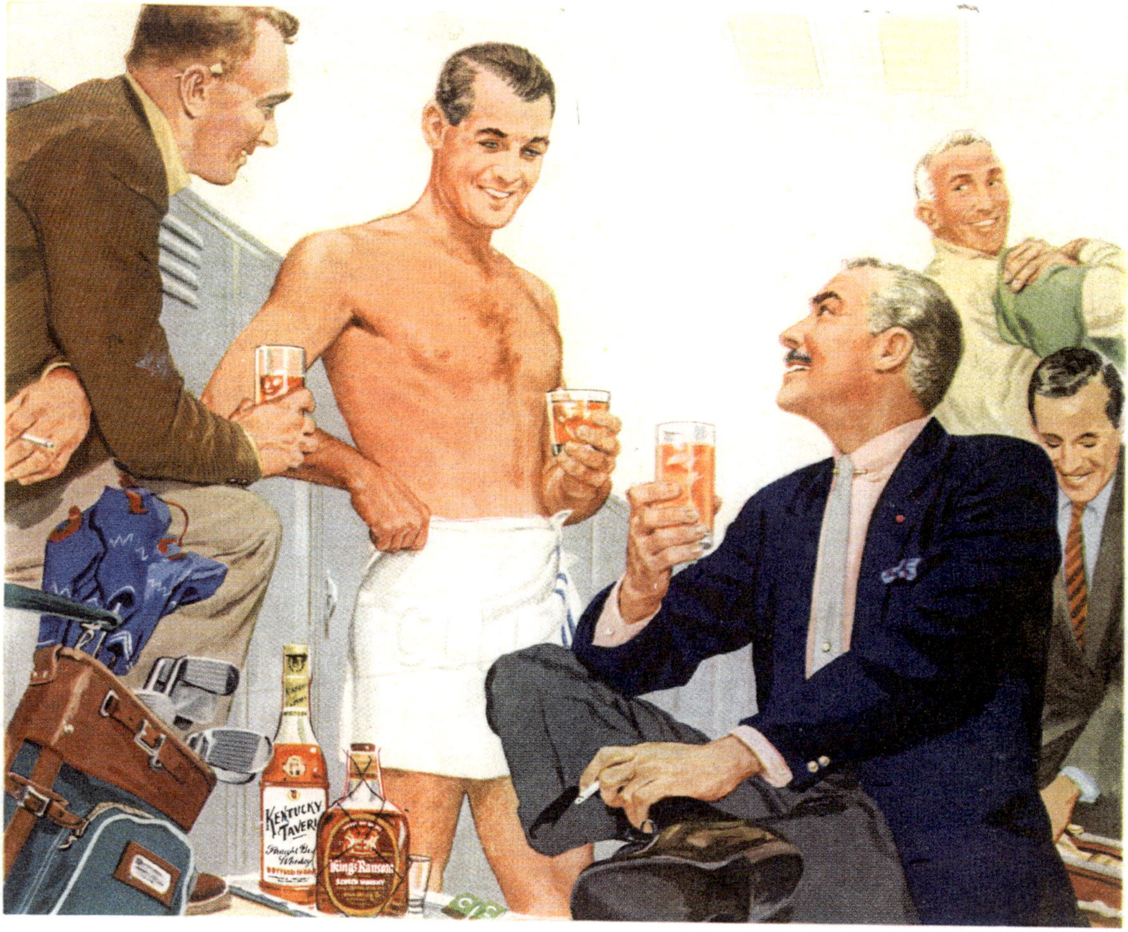

The Quality Whiskies to Serve…

FOR PEOPLE OF
INHERENT GOOD TASTE

KENTUCKY TAVERN

Outstanding among all Bonded Bourbons

The vigorous, velvety smoothness of Kentucky Tavern is legend. It's the top-quality premium Bonded Bourbon with a genuine Kentucky sour-mash flavor you'll cherish.
KENTUCKY STRAIGHT BOURBON WHISKEY. 100 PROOF, BOTTLED-IN-BOND

KING'S RANSOM
The Finest Scotch of all—Famed Round the World

To Scotch lovers everywhere this celebrated imported whisky stands for the very pinnacle of premium Scotch quality. It has a world-wide reputation for warmth and flavor that's unexcelled.
BLENDED SCOTCH WHISKY. 94 PROOF

HOUSE OF LORDS
The Lighter Scotch That's a Peer Among Whiskies

House of Lords imported Scotch is justly renowned as a slightly lighter and milder Scotch. For generation after generation its classic quality and taste have made it an irreplaceable favorite among Britain's Peerage.
BLENDED SCOTCH WHISKY. 86 PROOF

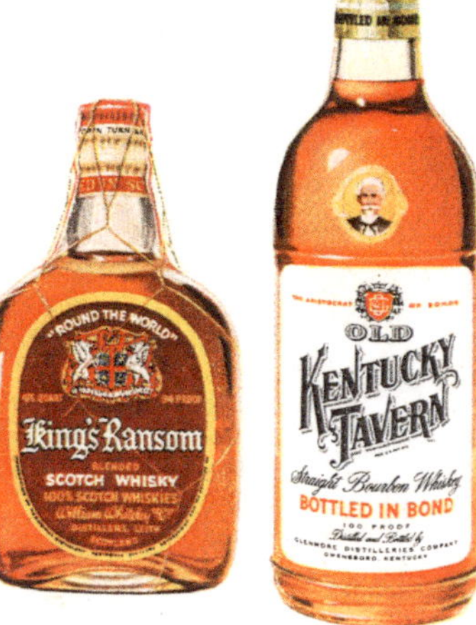
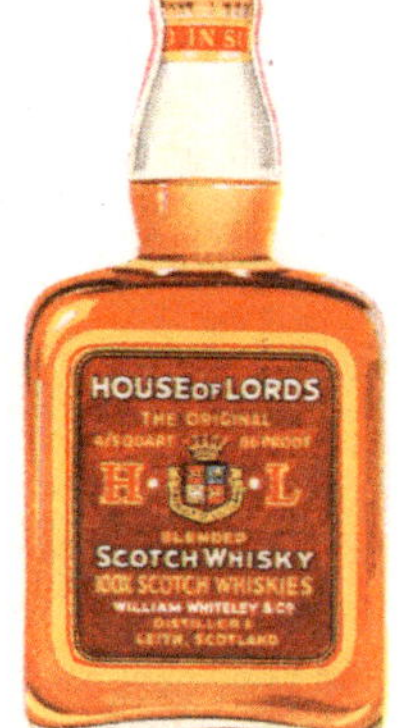

G L E N M O R E   D I S T I L L E R I E S   Company *"Where Perfection of Product is Tradition"*
LOUISVILLE, KENTUCKY

THE MALE "GAZE" IN HOMOEROTIC BOURBON HISTORY

Faulkner Morgan Archive *@faulknermorganachive*

Queer folks have often taken advantage of ambiguity as a way to get their images and fantasies before a wider audience. Advertisements, especially, have long served as a public-facing format to create such imagery. For instance, young men reading Time Magazine around the 1950s would have been greeted by ads like this one. Though meant to advertise the whiskies of Glenmore Distilleries, this ad looks more like the opening shot of a 1970s gay porn than a Bourbon ad. While they appear to be enjoying their whiskey in this locker room, there seems to be a lot more going on in this image.

The most pronounced visual aspect of this image is that the men are in different states of dressing & undressing. The central, shirtless figure is surrounded by clothed men in suits, creating a power dynamic between him and the rest of the men; he becomes something to be viewed, to be gazed upon. The ways in which the men are looking and gazing at each other also plays a major role in this scene, and this type of homoerotic, seductive eye contact can be seen in many Queer artists' work around this time. We can look to the illustrations of J.C. Leyendecker, the drawings of Paul Cadmus, and even the paintings of Kentucky-born artist Edward Melcarth to see the "gaze" as a prevalent marker of sexual interest between men. The importance of the gaze makes sense, too, when you think about the homosexual culture of the 1950s and 1960s. Much of the conversation at that time, especially when cruising and looking for sex, was nonverbal and depending on understanding different "looks."

This specific image is not an outlier either, but rather part of a long line of Glenmore Distilleries ads that invoke this, possibly not-so-subtle, homoeroticism. Glenmore's slogan, "for people of inherent good taste," placed in the context of these images implies that one's taste in Bourbon is not the only thing that matters. Instead, it implies that their Bourbon is meant for these high-class, masculine, wealthy men that are depicted, and can attract those of the same. As this ad shows, gay folks were there, living their lives, and having a laugh through subversive imagery like this.

At the Forefront of Queer Inclusive Bourbon: Old Forester

Queer Kentucky Staff

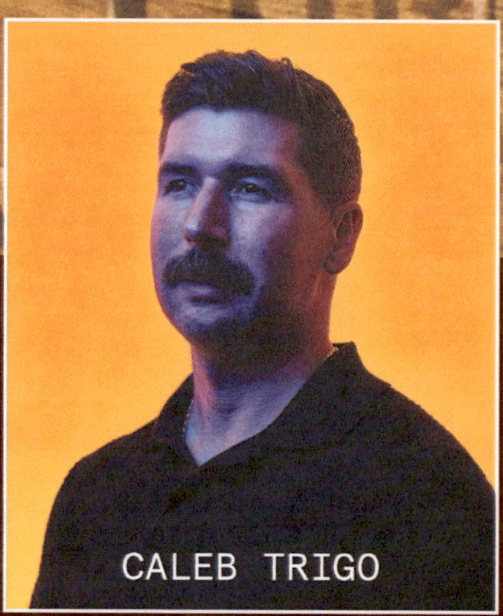

CALEB TRIGO

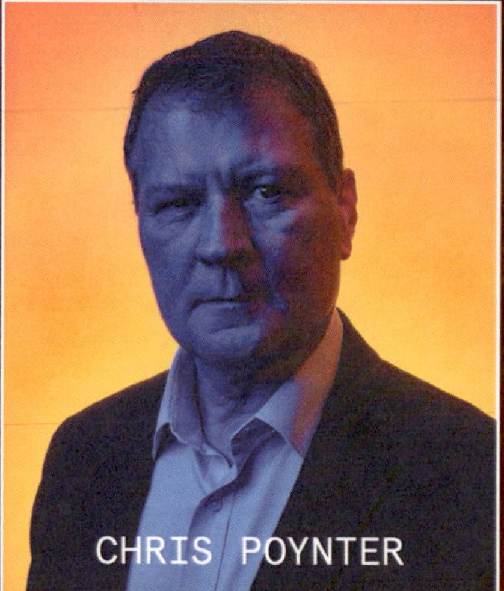

CHRIS POYNTER

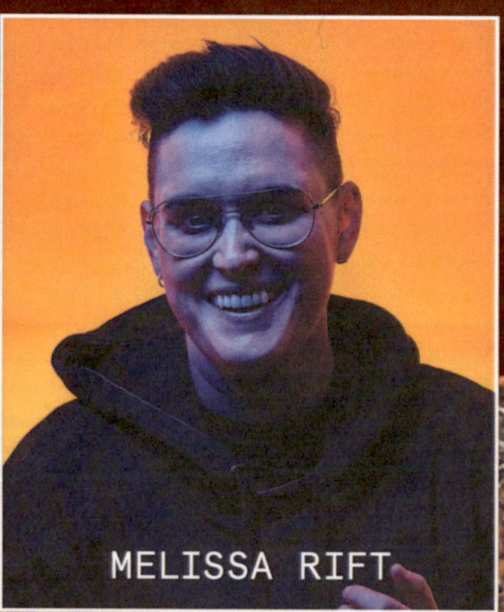

MELISSA RIFT

Images by Ryan Grant   he/him   @ryangrantphoto

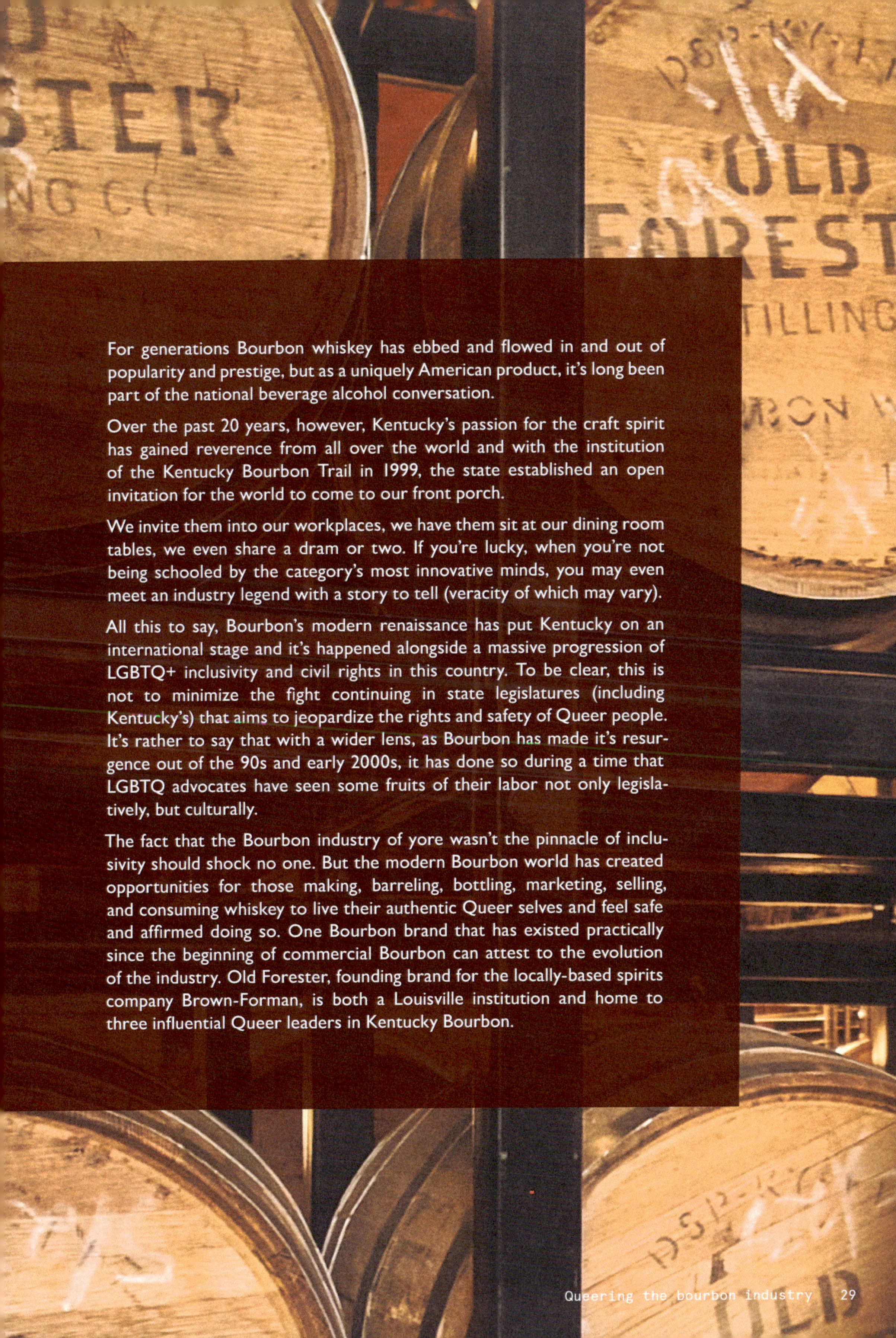

For generations Bourbon whiskey has ebbed and flowed in and out of popularity and prestige, but as a uniquely American product, it's long been part of the national beverage alcohol conversation.

Over the past 20 years, however, Kentucky's passion for the craft spirit has gained reverence from all over the world and with the institution of the Kentucky Bourbon Trail in 1999, the state established an open invitation for the world to come to our front porch.

We invite them into our workplaces, we have them sit at our dining room tables, we even share a dram or two. If you're lucky, when you're not being schooled by the category's most innovative minds, you may even meet an industry legend with a story to tell (veracity of which may vary).

All this to say, Bourbon's modern renaissance has put Kentucky on an international stage and it's happened alongside a massive progression of LGBTQ+ inclusivity and civil rights in this country. To be clear, this is not to minimize the fight continuing in state legislatures (including Kentucky's) that aims to jeopardize the rights and safety of Queer people. It's rather to say that with a wider lens, as Bourbon has made it's resurgence out of the 90s and early 2000s, it has done so during a time that LGBTQ advocates have seen some fruits of their labor not only legislatively, but culturally.

The fact that the Bourbon industry of yore wasn't the pinnacle of inclusivity should shock no one. But the modern Bourbon world has created opportunities for those making, barreling, bottling, marketing, selling, and consuming whiskey to live their authentic Queer selves and feel safe and affirmed doing so. One Bourbon brand that has existed practically since the beginning of commercial Bourbon can attest to the evolution of the industry. Old Forester, founding brand for the locally-based spirits company Brown-Forman, is both a Louisville institution and home to three influential Queer leaders in Kentucky Bourbon.

CALEB TRIGO

One of the industry's burning questions from the outside world is how do you get to work on whiskey. Bourbon fans want a curriculum and a road map to realizing their lifelong dream of working on their favorite Bourbon brand, but with such a multifaceted industry there are endless points of entry. However, when it comes to actually making the spirit, Caleb Trigo is a pretty good example of how to school your way into some pretty incredible opportunities. Trigo currently works as the senior engineering manager for Brown-Forman Brands and was named the Assistant Master Distiller for Old Forester earlier this year.

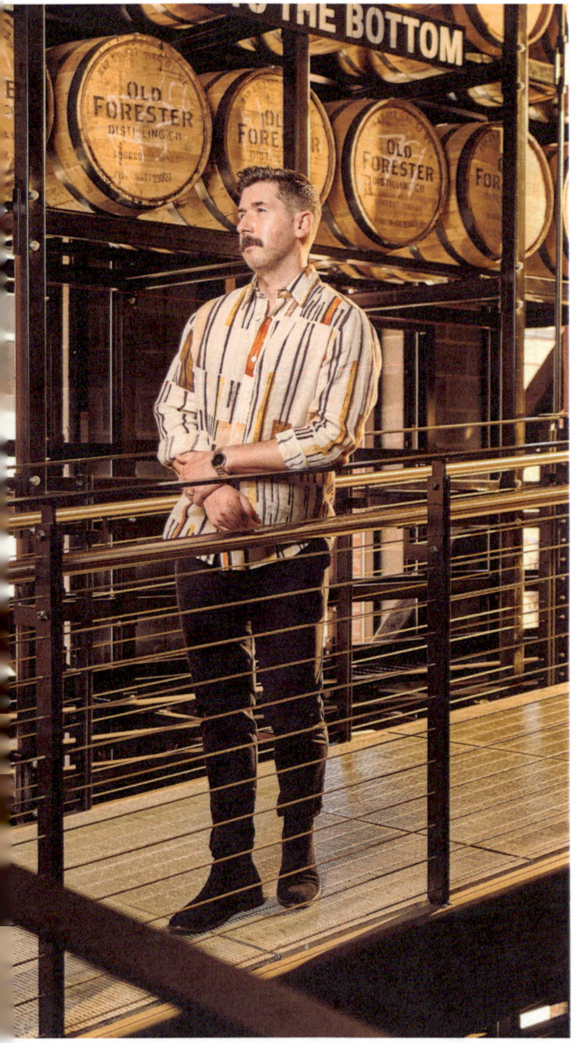

After growing up in a small town in Western Kentucky, Trigo found his way to Louisville to attend the University of Louisville's Speed School of Engineering. He landed at Brown-Forman's Process Research and Development department as a school co-op requirement, later leading to a full-time role with the company after completing his degree. Trigo later completed a master's degree in brewing and distilling from Heriot-Watt University in Scotland. Not only has he held numerous positions in R&D, operations management, and engineering for Kentucky Bourbon brands, but he recently took a job opportunity in Panama City integrating newly acquired Diplomatico Rum into Brown-Forman's portfolio. Products Trigo has touched have gone into stores and behind bars all over the globe at this point.

He says that being Queer and open in the workplace has never really created a barrier during his time at Brown-Forman. After facing challenges with acceptance from his family, Trigo says his "chosen family quickly grew both in [his] personal life and at work.

"Brown-Forman was such an amazing place to be coming-out in that I immediately got involved with the PRIDE group and met so many amazing people," he explained.

PRIDE is an established employee resource group at the company in which Trigo has held leadership roles in addition to engaging with several diversity and inclusion initiatives company-wide.

Though Trigo has found confidence in being his authentic self while getting to make delicious spirits day in and out, we can't assume this is the experience of all Queer people in the industry, and certainly hasn't been historically. But Queer visibility in the Bourbon industry in particular is on the rise.

"The Bourbon industry is evolving in parallel with many other legacy industries — thus, change is inherent and imperative," he says. "With that, as the Queer community grows so does its presence in our company and industry."

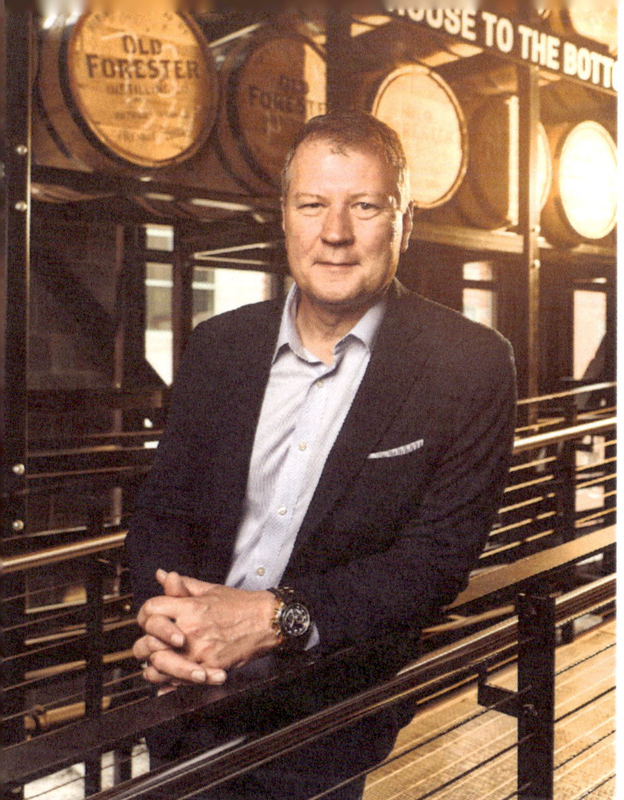

CHRIS POYNTER

While Trigo represents the side of the industry making the whiskey, others do the work of making sure people discover it. Chris Poynter is the public relations and partnership manager for both Old Forester and Woodford Reserve at Brown-Forman. Born in Bourbon County, he says Bourbon is in his blood.

Having grown up in rural Kentucky in the 1970s and 80s, he says that he never knowingly experienced discrimination outside of the occasional high school insult. And when he came out? It was a surprise to no one.

"The only obstacles I've faced are those I've created for myself — I think most people can relate to that," he says. Poynter has found his friends and family to always be a cornerstone of love, support, and personal growth in his life.

In a field like public relations, Poynter is partially tasked with communicating to the masses a brand's story. After beginning his work on Woodford Reserve six years ago, and Old Forester three years ago, Poynter touts Brown-Forman's affirming workplace culture.

"Brown-Forman (and the spirits industry in general) is open and welcoming to everyone, gay or straight," he says. "We were one of the first companies in Kentucky to earn 100 percent on the Human Rights Campaign corporate scorecard. Other businesses can learn from our company's inclusive culture."

At the age of 53, Poynter has seen, firsthand, the evolution of both bourbon culture and LGBTQ acceptance that Trigo alluded to.

"I hope that younger people can look at me, see my success and know that being gay is not an obstacle in life, but a positive". Poynter adds, "Being gay, after all, is only one part of who I am."

MELISSA RIFT

A third and entirely different but integral side of the Bourbon industry is hospitality. Not everything you might market to consumers has an element of hospitality, but selling Kentucky Bourbon is selling hospitality.

Melissa Rift, master taster and brand ambassador for Old Forester found their way to bourbon through the Kentucky Bourbon Trail

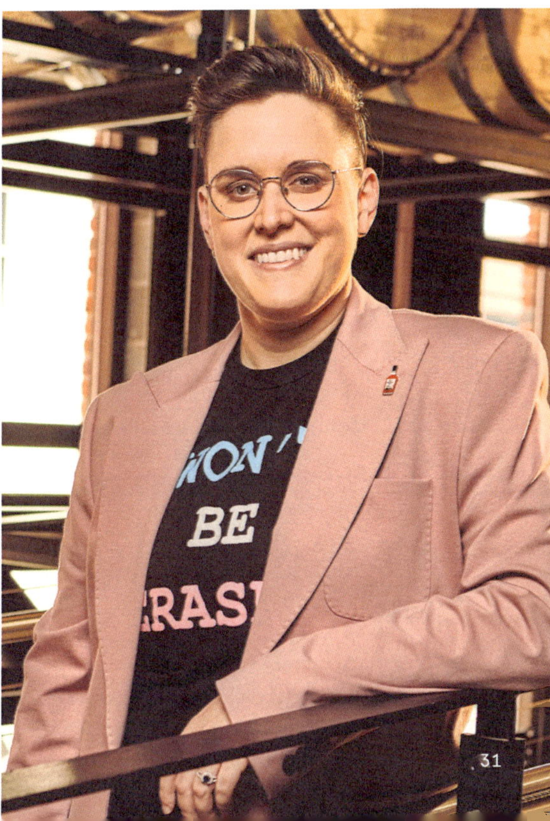

and hospitality. After beginning as a tour guide at a distillery, they ended up managing a private single barrel program where they would both sell whiskey and build relationships with a vast network of industry partners, clients and customers.

"As a point of origin, this served really well to give me a foundational bourbon education and learn how to teach people about bourbon," Rift says about their career.

When a job for master taster of their favorite brand opened up, they jumped at the opportunity.

"Everyone's first question is what does a master taster do."

Rift describes their role with Old Forester as two-pronged. Half of the role is the "taster" part, which involves continued quality assurance and product innovation. The other half is acting as a conduit between the brand marketing team and the sales force and consumers. Rift, whose educational background is actually in family therapy and not distilled spirits, says they've "always enjoyed cross-functional positions that connect multiple teams within a company." Their freedom to be their authentic self has certainly contributed to their success in this regard.

When it comes to being Queer in the industry, Rift feels they haven't experienced any "overt obstacles" because of their identity.

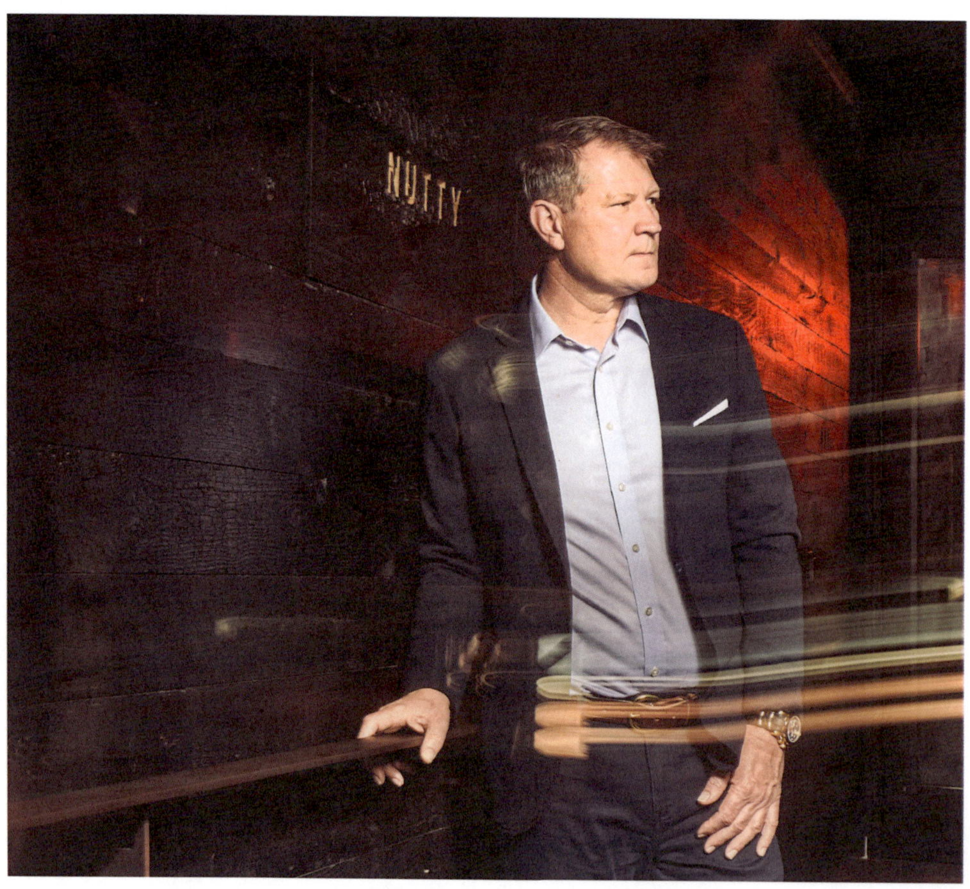

I THINK WE COULD DO BETTER WITH THAT."

Melissa Rift

"There are of course microaggressions, lack of visibility and a definite lack of consideration when it comes to being not only Queer but gender-fluid," they said. Rift adds that they will often be interviewed about what it's like to be a "woman in whiskey."

"It's still just a very binary space. I think we could do better with that."

For Rift, working in the whiskey industry is all about community.

"There is so much community to be had. It really does reach beyond a full-time job," Rift says. They not only find support from the bourbon community, but from their local Queer community as well.

An interesting theme in the history of Kentucky Bourbon is that of resilience. Through revolutions, rebellions, prohibitions, wars, natural disasters…Kentucky Bourbon has always found a way to persevere. So too has the Queer Community in this country and in this state.

There have always been Queer people in Kentucky, and there have always been Queer people working in bourbon. Representation matters, so it matters when people like Trigo, Poynter and Rift do the jobs they do and give visibility to that.

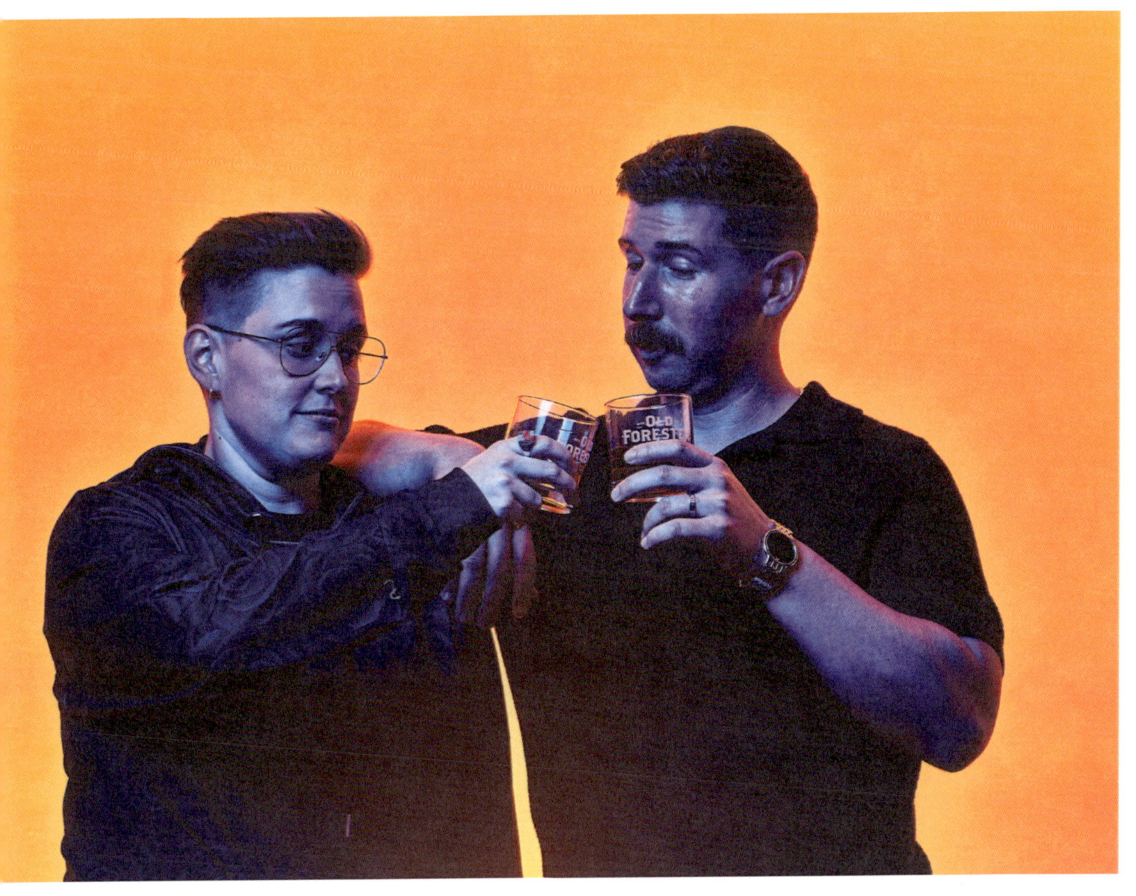

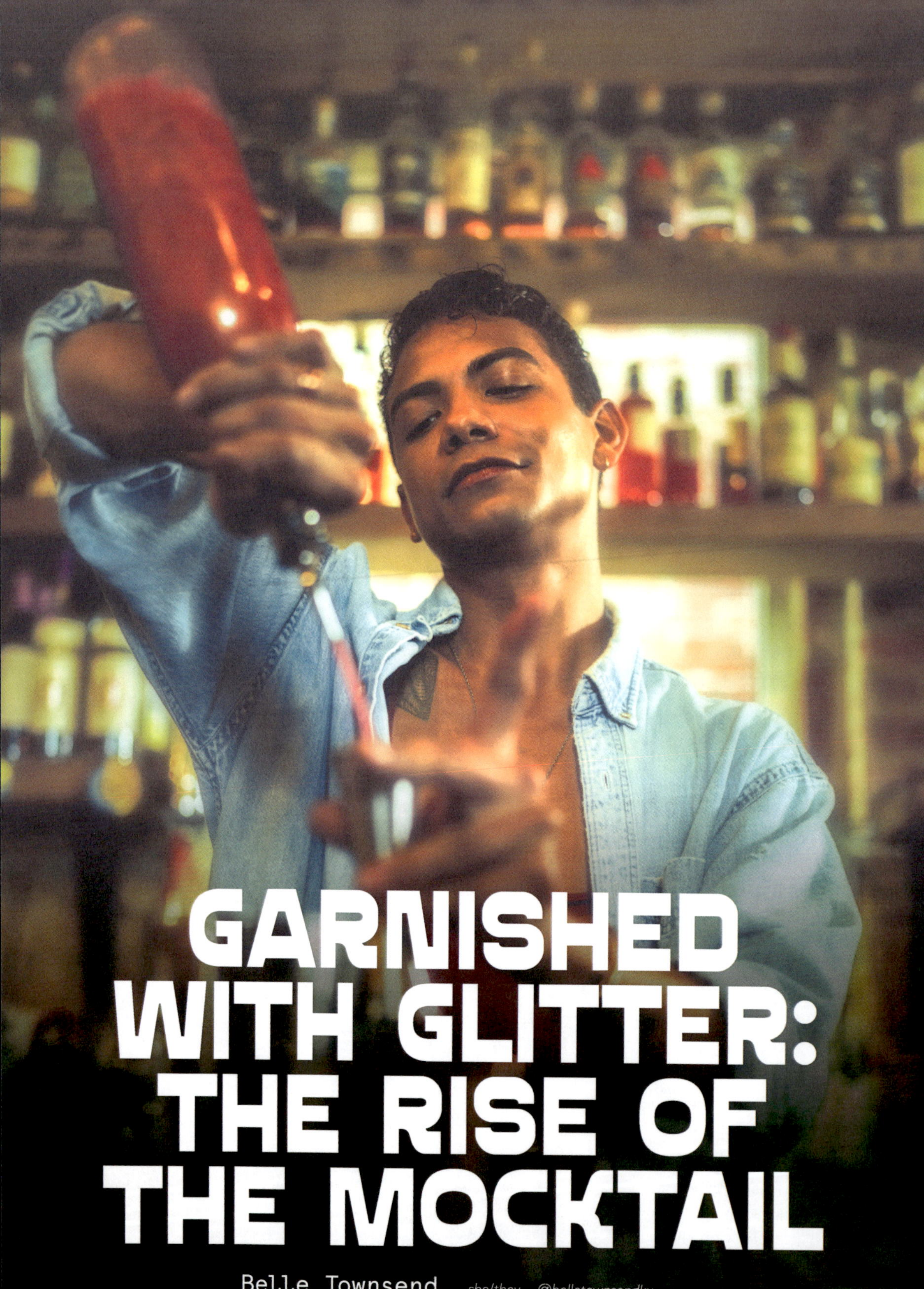

Belle Townsend   she/they   @belletownsendky

THE BOOZE BEGINNING

I did not grow up with Queer people around me in rural Kentucky. But, I did have a fabulous, good country woman as a grandmother. She taught me how to cook, how to be myself no matter what anyone thought, and how to fight to survive in a world that punishes those of us who lean into being fearlessly embellished.

This is to say that I inherited much of myself from her. After she passed away when I was 15, I was surprised to learn that she was an alcoholic for my entire life. I say this not to shame her or judge her. I pay tribute to what she survived every single day, but I have also had to reckon how I was taught to survive.

When I first went to college in Boston in 2018, I felt freer to be in Queer community. There were many nights where I made some of the best memories of my life, and there were more nights that I do not remember. I spent a lot of time at gay bars. These spaces felt safe for my friends and me, but I began noticing negative impacts. My chronic pain was worse. I was spending money I did not have to spare. I did multiple things that would leave me waking up embarrassed, apologizing to my friends for things I could barely remember, and partaking in the classic "hair of the dog" just to keep it movin'.

It was around this time that I reckoned I inherited much more than my grandma's fiery spirit.

Over the last three years, I have cyclically decreased my drinking, passively picked it back up, had things get out of control, and tried again to get a grip. It's been an excuse for me to drop out of reality and responsibility, as well as a coping mechanism. It's also constantly around me, as going out with my Queer friends usually means chugging a few vodka red bulls (sugar free, if they got it).

THE BOOZE RECKONING

In early February, I decided to fully quit drinking for the first time in my life. I did this in coordination with the 2024 Kentucky legislative session starting, knowing that I would be covering the anti-LGBTQ+ legislation for Queer Kentucky as their political correspondent. I first covered these topics in 2023's session, and it took an incredible toll on my mental health.

The rhetoric of this legislation is cruel and violent. While I knew this coverage was necessary for our community to know how we are being targeted, I also could see the devastating impacts of this legislation on my community. It has weighed on me tremendously, as I know it has for anyone in the LGBTQ+ community and for those who love us. In the 2023 legislative session, I noticed that I returned to my cycle of drinking. This was oftentimes with other Queer people: activists, organizers, and people who understood the reality our community was and is facing.

For the 2024 legislative session, I did not want to give my spirit and health to the politicians and syndicates pushing this legislation. So, I quit drinking. And, I have been sober from alcohol since.

It has been difficult. In addition to the addictive tendencies I inherited, part of the difficulty comes from still wanting to go out and be social. This is why I was so excited when I learned that somewhere I liked to go when I was still drinking, Trouble Bar, offered $1 mocktails of most of their drinks.

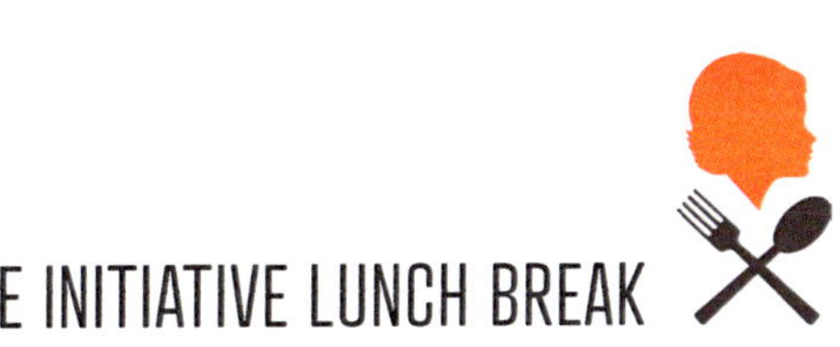

BEYOND THE BOOZE

Nicole Stipp and Kaitlyn Owens, co-owners, have had family members and friends who have struggled with substance abuse. So, Trouble Bar was created as a space that would accommodate their lived experiences. Stipp shares, "Part of our inexpensive non-alcoholic beverage program is because we view Trouble Bar as a third space that we hope you can engage with in a large or small monetary exchange – or even none at all!"

The owners believe that third spaces, "a gathering point that is neither work nor home," are hard to come by. Part of the accessibility of the third space includes having "movable furniture, a mobility-impaired accessible space, and a staff of kind, friendly folks who are all a part of making the bar a place where people want to come together."

Half of the ownership of Trouble Bar is Queer, and day-to-day, they see a lot of Queer patrons. Nicole still believes this is due to intentionally designing "our hiring process, our menu, and our physical space to be centered on being welcoming and kind."

She continues, "You can hang up all the Queer art and Queer flags you want, but if your staff don't welcome ALL folks in with open arms, that mission is much harder to accomplish."

Stipp points to the last few years as reminding us that loneliness can wreak havoc on our society, and how "it's an honor to be able to create a space that folks feel like they can come and socialize no matter their interest or ability to consume alcohol."

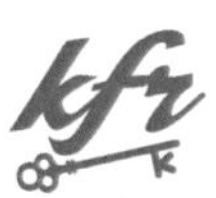

Founder of Kentucky based brand KFR, Kasey Guelda, shares that his time during lockdown was where he reflected on his overconsumption of alcohol. Through making different functional beverages at home as a hobby as an alternative to alcohol, sugary soda, or vinegar-like tasting kombucha, Guelda came across water kefir. A probiotic, fermented, non-alcoholic drink, KFR's water kefir has up to 3x the amount of probiotics as kombucha and 2 grams of sugar or less depending on the flavor.

Guelda grew up in the gay scene, and this involved lots of drinking alcohol. While he acknowledges there were other facets of gay life, this was what the media and his peers showed him.

"My days were consumed with looking cute, getting f'd up at the bar, and where the next party was," he says.

Guelda felt cut off from some Queer community when he quit drinking. "Having enjoyable alternatives makes everyone feel like they can be included in those spaces," he says.

Eric Wentworth and J.D. Mitchell, co-founders of the Kentucky based cocktail and mocktail mixer-making business Modica, expressed similar sentiment in wanting to have options that were inclusive. As gay men, the owners know that gay bars were an important space for Queer people, and that Queer people tend to drink more than other demographics.

Their offerings not only make conscious intake and sobriety more fun and accessible, but also full of flavor and full of far less sugar than other mocktail options.

"Although we both drink alcohol, we take breaks frequently and we're often looking for non-alc options that are just as delicious and elevated as the cocktails we're used to. We love working with gay bars to offer Modica mocktails so anyone who isn't drinking doesn't feel left out, or doesn't feel like the only option is juice or soda," says Wentworth and Mitchell.

They continue to share that mindset is everything, because, "if you know why you're doing something, especially if it's for your long-term health, is great motivation for making a change."

It is because of folks attempting to make sobriety inclusive and accessible that this pursuit has been far less lonely for me than it otherwise would be. It's because of my own motivation as well as people like them that I have learned I do not have to blackout in order to have fun, let go, and shake some ass.

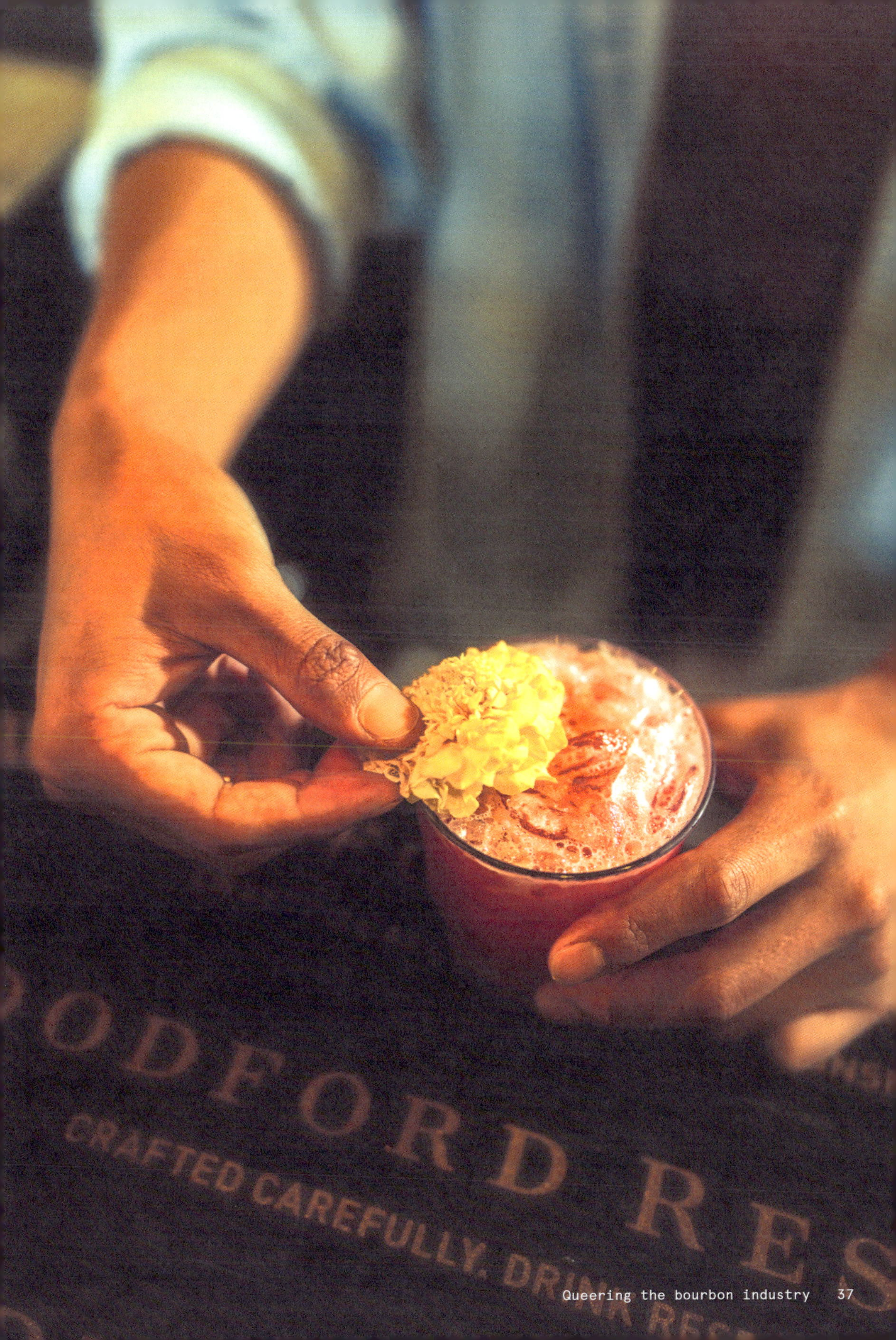

WOODFORD RES
CRAFTED CAREFULLY. DRINK RES

STRAIGHT UP GAY ENTREPRENEUR ROCKS THE BOURBON TOURISM INDUSTRY

Spencer Adkins
he/him   @therealspenceradkins

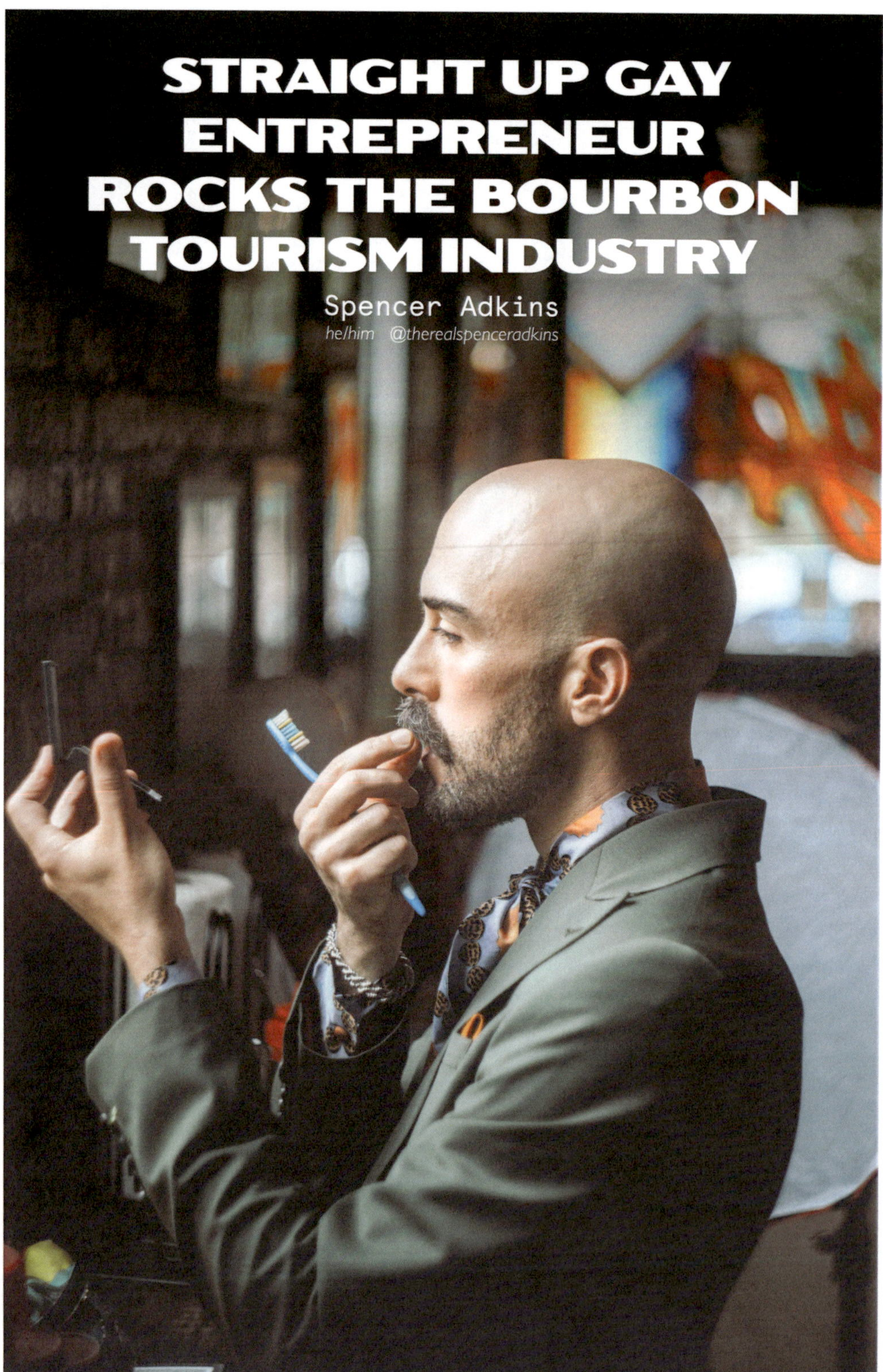

Images by Reed Sampley   he/him   @reedsampley

Eddie Fieldhouse dunks a tea bag into hot water as he sits across from me in a Louisville coffee house. We're both a bit windswept and wet from the rain, and he settles into our warm corner as we begin to talk Bourbon.

"Oh, God," he stammered when asked his favorite Bourbon. Of course, he couldn't easily pick one. "It depends on what I'm doing and who I'm with. One of the ones that stands out to me right now is Dark Arts. Any of that lineup of products."

His qualifications? Eddie Fieldhouse is the co-founder and CEO of Kentucky Hug, a centralized booking platform for Bourbon experiences. Whether it be distillery tours or tastings, Fieldhouse knows his Bourbon.

"So, there's two audiences for the Kentucky Hug: there's the distillery and the people who want to go visit the distillery." He explains that the average Bourbon tourist is spending six to eight hours sifting through around a hundred distillery options on Google. That's just for tours — it doesn't include tastings or events ("any of the cool stuff that goes in and around Bourbon").

Previously, if users couldn't afford to spend eight hours researching their Bourbon Trail excursion, their next best option was to pay a tour company hundreds – or even thousands – of dollars to efficiently book and arrange the itinerary. The average tourist, however, doesn't have the time or money for these avenues.

Enter the Kentucky Hug: all users need to do is put in the dates they're traveling, and how many are in their party. Then, once they add their chosen experiences to their cart, the Kentucky Hug will build their trip for them at a small booking fee. "And you're not five clicks-deep on twenty-five different websites on twenty-five different tabs," Fieldhouse said.

His inspiration for the Kentucky Hug came from his frustration with distilleries' old-fashioned bookkeeping. Between lost reservations, unanswered phones, and outdated information, Bourbon's infrastructure wasn't able to keep up with its growth, but the Kentucky Hug streamlines this process and allows the average Bourbon enthusiast – the one without eight hours to kill – the opportunity to experience the pulse of American history for themselves.

He describes tourists running around downtown Bardstown trying to make it to their next reservation – running past all of the local, family-owned businesses that support this industry, the culture-keepers of this tradition.

"Bourbon is America's only native spirit. It should be as accessible as any museum on the National Mall in D.C., and yet it's not," he said. That is the heart of the Kentucky Hug: centering the average Bourbon consumer in the conversation."

The mom-and-pop businesses, the person on the factory line dipping the bottle - they're all just as important as the master distiller. "Those people both have stories going multiple generations back within the distilling industry. Both are valid and both are just as interesting when you go back to L.A. and tell someone about your trip here."

Fieldhouse's vision extends further than just commercial tourism, because it's "way beyond just Bourbon because Bourbon is context – it's community." He's seen firsthand how increased access to tourism in our rural communities of Kentucky help the people in those towns grow, learn, and combat isolationism.

Ten years ago, he was prepared to lead his first tour for a group of eight guests from California.

"I was so excited, I mean, I hadn't slept for days. I had practiced all this history and memorized everything." That is, until he experienced what many Queer people have before: the woman who was charged with letting tour groups into

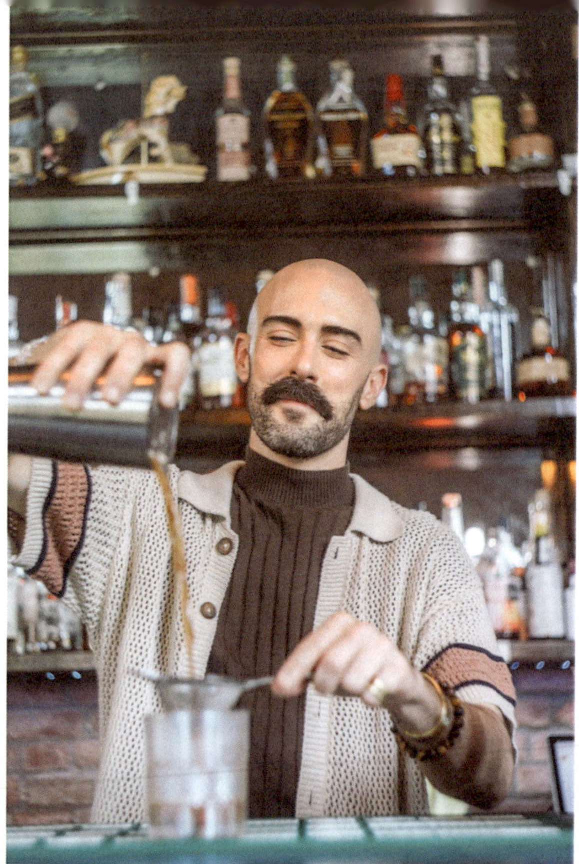

the distillery, named Julie, refused to look him in the eye, and continued to give him dirty looks. Eventually, to his embarrassment, Eddie and the guests who hired him were asked to leave the property. His Queerness was, apparently, making the staff uncomfortable.

Only two years later, Julie is giving her spiel to his tour group and asks for everyone's preferred pronouns. The rest of the visit went off without a hitch. She had no diversity equity and inclusion training, no managerial intervention – she simply had access and exposure, and through that, learned how to engage with people outside of her community.

"What was beautiful about it was that through her just engaging with people who were different from her, she learned and she changed her perspective," says Fieldhouse.

To a lot of people, Bourbon is seen as a boys' club. It feels overwhelmingly white, cisgendered, straight, and unwelcoming. Fieldhouse argues that this is, in part, because of the industry's lack of infrastructure and access – which is what he is providing through the Kentucky

Hug – and the people in the Bourbon industry aren't as immutable as we might think.

"Everyone has the opportunity to change. Nothing is permanent. If we can make small towns more accessible in a way that's safe for both parties – that gives both parties autonomy – the world's guaranteed to be a better place. I've seen it get better."

At the end of the day, Bourbon is much more than just a drink; it's Kentucky's legacy. "Generational histories change over time. It's the story of people – a story of community. I want people to see that, and I feel like if we had a way of looking at it that wasn't so clouded with advertising, we'd be able to touch it easier." By making these experiences accessible, Fieldhouse is sharing the traditions of ordinary Kentuckians.

Dan Murphy, executive director of Slingshot Ventures, which is the startup and innovation arm of the software development company Slingshot, has supported the backend of the Kentucky Hug since its inception.

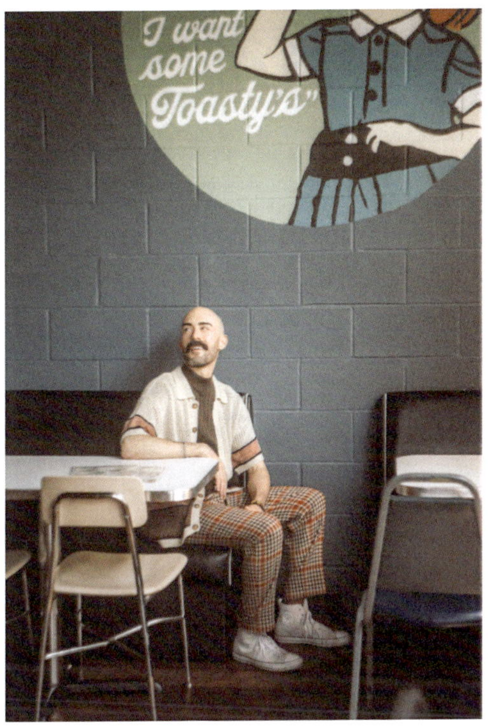

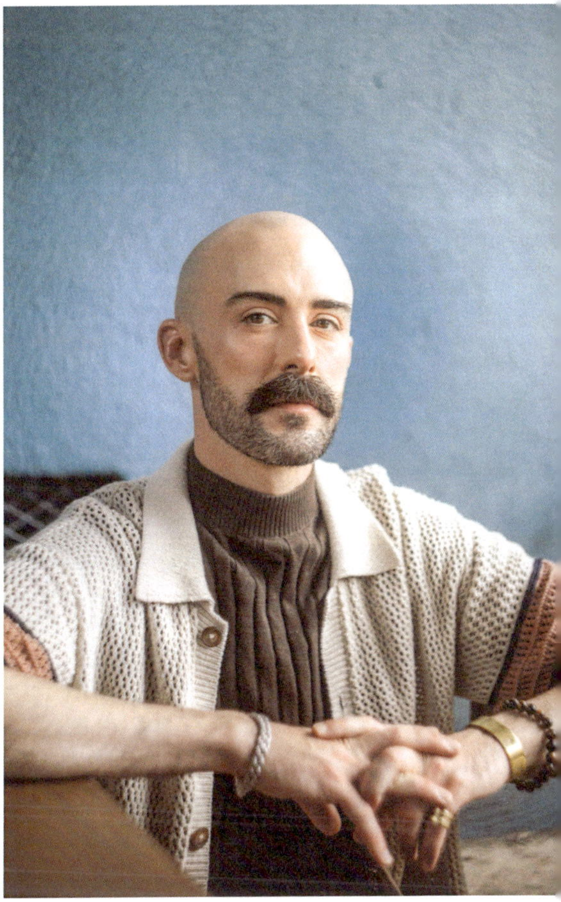

"Working with Eddie has been eye opening," says Murphy. "Some of his [stories] encapsulate a lot of things I'm not familiar with, so I'm learning a lot in that regard. It's fun to watch him learn."

Slingshot, based in Louisville, helps new entrepreneurs get their businesses up and running.

"With anybody starting something new, they want it. But understanding what it takes to get it is completely different, and I think it can be a shell shock for entrepreneurs," Murphy said.

He tells me, illustrating the trepidation new business owners face, "You can see the human element - the learning something new and struggling with not being efficient at it quickly. There's a growing up that I think happens."

This same hesitance of uncharted territory has allowed Fieldhouse the opportunity to grow in new ways. "He was engaging with the industry in one way, and now he's looking at it a different way," he says before making a point to say, "It's not an issue. It's a learning curve."

According to Murphy, the Kentucky Hug has the momentum to make Bourbon tourism accessible. "I don't think any of us were necessarily aware of how big what we're doing is. It's an ambitious, lofty goal, but there's no reason we can't do it." He then referenced Bourbon and Belonging directly, echoing Fieldhouse's vision for the Kentucky Hug: "Helping the distilleries is one thing, but being able to elevate communities … like with the event in October - that is why we're doing what we're doing."

It's not often that you come across someone with a vision as strong and clear as Eddie Fieldhouse. Fed up with old-fashioned infrastructure and the high barrier to entry, he set out to do what no one else could do, because only a Kaintuck could do it. Streamlining the Bourbon industry is no small undertaking. He is a trailblazer, put simply — a keeper of Bourbon tradition, and an impressive businessman.

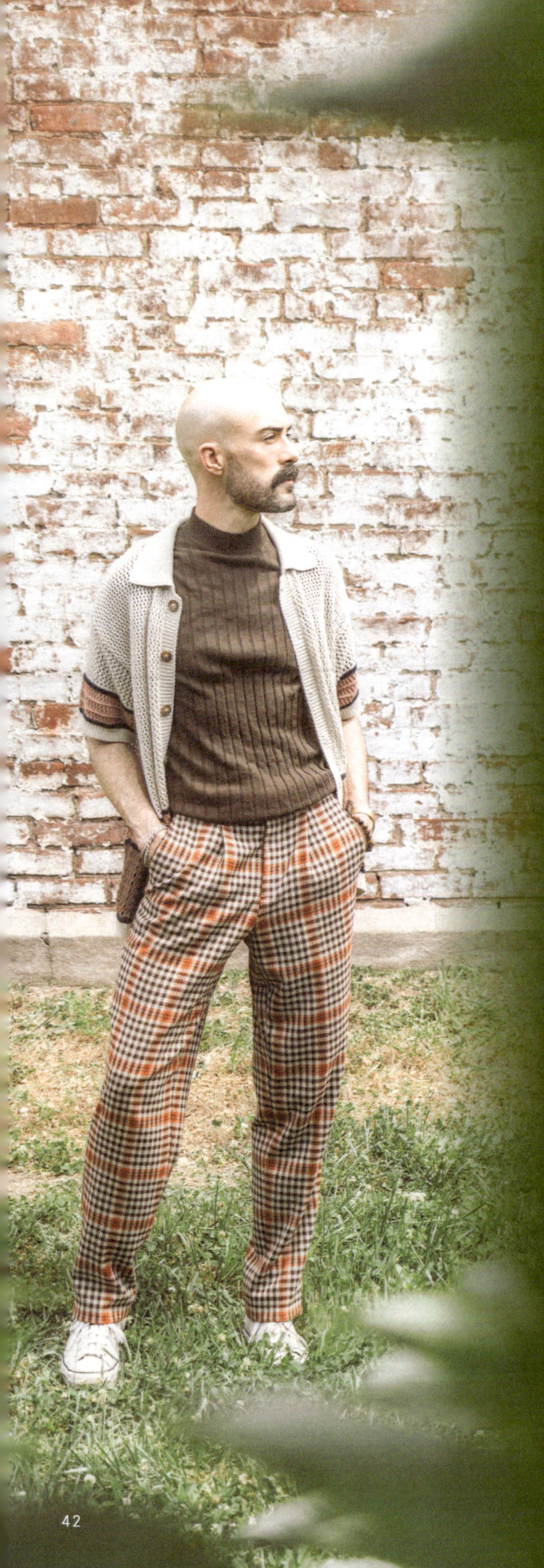

ITINERARY

FRIDAY

Staying in NULU or Germantown, depending on the group.

SATURDAY

9AM: Eat breakfast (he couldn't stress this enough) at Wiltshire Pantry, Louisville

11AM: Beam Made Bourbon Distillery Tour & Tasting at the Jim Beam Distilling Co., Clermont

1PM: lunch reservation at The Bar at Willett, Bardstown

3:30PM: Old Forester Tour, Louisville

5PM: Angel's Envy Whiskey Connoisseur Tasting, Louisville

7:30PM: dinner reservation at Enso, Louisville

NIGHTCAP at Hilltop Tavern, Louisville

SUNDAY

10:45AM: Leo Moo Drag Brunch, Louisville

1:30PM: Evan Williams Traditional Tour & Tasting, Louisville

3:30PM: The Copper & Kings Experience – rooftop cocktails to follow tour, Louisville

7:00PM: dinner reservation at Decade, Louisville

NIGHTCAP at Play Louisville

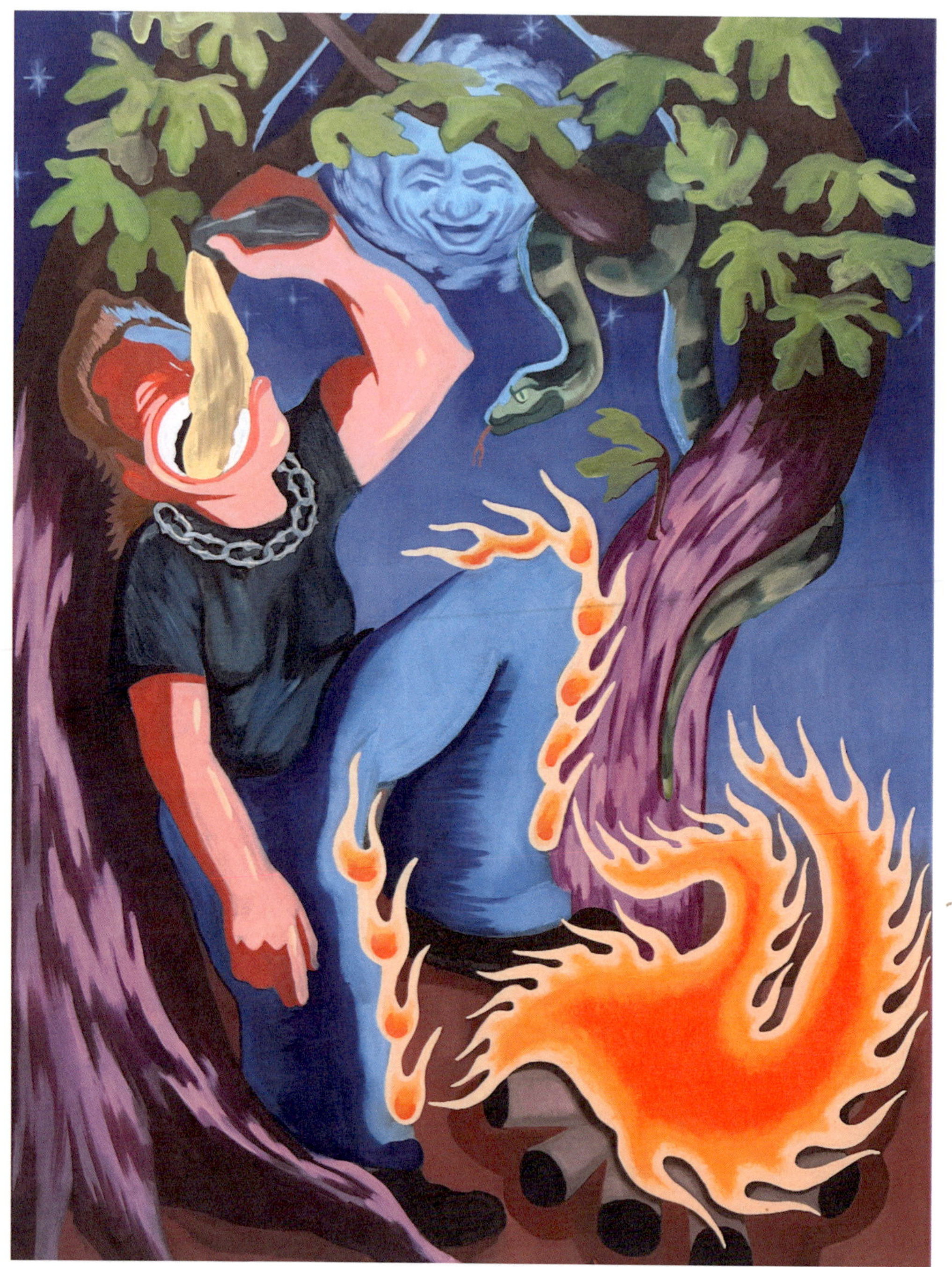

PERSONALIZED RECOVERY

GAY SOUTHERN KENTUCKY MEN SHARE
THEIR ONGOING PATHS TO RECOVERY

Will Whaley *he/him* @willwhaleyjpg

Artwork by Ceirra Evans   she/her   @ceirra_evans

The path of addiction and recovery is not linear.

That is something that Lucas Blackburn and Josh Shaw can attest to in their recovery journeys.

Currently, Blackburn has been sober for nearly four years, and Shaw has been sober for six and a half years. Despite this, it wasn't always this way.

The two gay men grew up in the South: Blackburn from Old Hickory, Tennessee, and Shaw from Munfordville.

Alcohol was something that the two men said they were used to being around, but they themselves did not start drinking until their 20s. Blackburn says one of his co-workers started buying alcohol for him, and he could tell within a year of drinking that he knew he was an alcoholic.

In 2002, Blackburn was admitted to the hospital where he remained sober for 30 days.

Blackburn met his partner in 2003, and by the end of that year, he wanted Blackburn to move in with him with the terms that he quit drinking.

"I finally went to a 12 step program in April 2004," he said, adding that he stayed with the program for a year, and then spent two years on his own before relapsing again.

In 2008, Blackburn and his partner moved to Louisiana, where he started another program before another relapse.

From 2011 to 2020, Blackburn went to eight different rehabs, never staying sober for more than six months.

It wasn't until the couple moved to Bowling Green that he was able to complete a 12 step program and stick to it.

Shaw says he grew up around alcohol and drugs, as his family members were users. When he was younger, his goal was to not follow in their footsteps.

At 19, he started drinking, and started going to clubs and bars in Louisville.

Shaw says alcohol gave him the push to go on the dance floor, sing karaoke, and interact with other gay men.

At 22, Shaw experienced heartbreak and used alcohol to cope.

At 29, he started recovery for the first time.

The breaking point was when Shaw's mother told him to leave after he had driven to her home under the influence. That was the moment he decided to seek help.

"She'd never done that before," he said. "It came across me … if I don't do something right now, my life's not going to get any better."

Shaw completed 30 days in a rehab and went to stay at a Sober Living Home. He moved out a year later, but continued going to meetings.

He started college at Bowling Green Tech working on his general education classes.

He made friends there and began going out with them to bars.

Shaw said he would drink RedBulls.

"I was a year and a half sober and I decided at a drag show to have a shot of whiskey," he said.

This was when his addiction gradually made its way back into Shaw's life, and drinking became the main focus again as he attended Western Kentucky University.

Eventually Shaw returned to the same program he had been through before.

He graduated from WKU with his bachelor's degree and completed his program steps.

Shaw lived in a Sober Living House again and worked part time at a Zaxby's in order to have a work schedule that allowed him to have meetings with his sponsor.

At this point he had five DUIs and was driving a scooter.

"I was battling my ego everyday, thinking I deserve better," he said.

Shaw then went to get his master's degree and worked as a therapist for the center that he started recovery in.

Shaw and Blackburn both now sponsor others recovering. Shaw's professional career works with those in recovery as well.

Blackburn said sponsoring others in recovery helps himself as well as the people he sponsors.

Shaw and Blackburn are not alone in their struggles.

Those in the LGBTQ community statistically face higher odds to have substance addictions.

Mithra Salmassi, the Educational Content Editor for Partnership to End Addiction, a nonprofit that works to provide support to families of those who might be going through addiction, said research shows the LGBTQ community is twice as likely to use substances over their heterosexual peers.

Salmassi said that trans individuals and LGBTQ people of color are even more at risk.

Salmassi cites SAMHSA, The Substance Abuse and Mental Health Services Administration, who puts out national surveys on drug use and health every year.

Salmassi said the 2021-2022 survey only looked at sexual minority individuals, but did not include non-binary or trans individuals.

"They found that sexual minority individuals, who are 18 and older, are more likely to have had a substance use disorder in the past year," she said. "About a third of bisexual males, bisexual females and gay males have had a substance abuse disorder in the past year, almost twice as likely to have been heavy drinkers, two to three times more likely to use marijuana and are twice as likely to have misused stimulants like cocaine and meth."

Salmassi said that data has only recently been collected studying the abuse habits of the LGBTQ community, adding that there has been a lack of specialized services for those needs.

"For trans individuals, a big problem is inpatient treatment," she said, adding that there's a lack of gender neutral facilities.

However, the situation is improving.

"I think there's more training for professionals on working with the LGBTQ population," she said. "There is definitely a movement, especially in the past few years, as people have become more aware of the particulars of someone's identity, especially a marginalized individual. I would say we are generally moving in a good direction."

Salmassi, Shaw, and Blackburn encourage LGBTQ individuals struggling with addiction to seek help.

"Don't feel like you have to adapt to what other people are doing," said Shaw. "Recovery is personalized. It really is."

"In order for us to get sober, we have to admit that we have a problem," Blackburn said.

> *"Don't feel like you have to adapt to what other people are doing," said Shaw. "Recovery is personalized. It really is."*

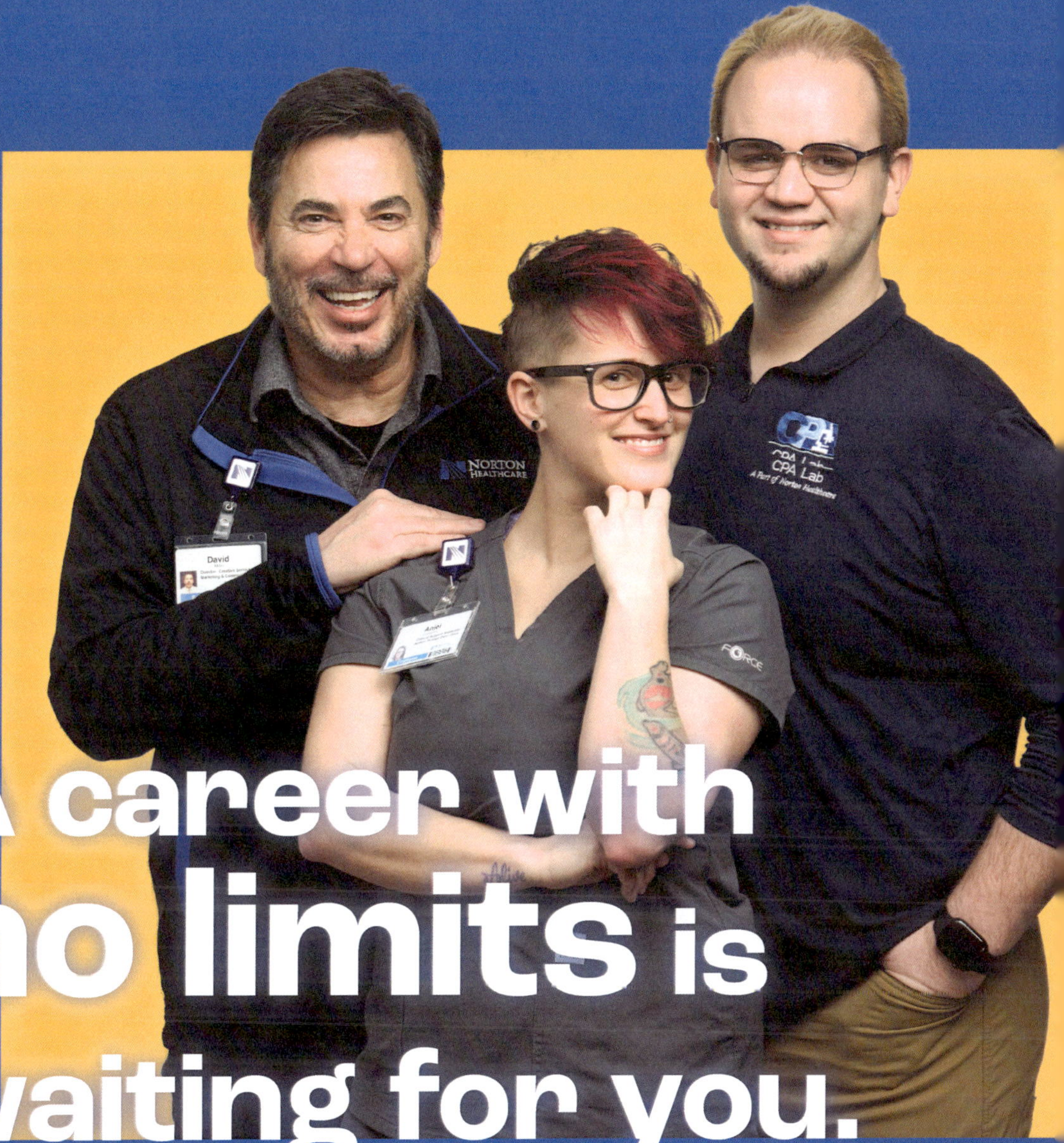

A career with no limits is waiting for you.

Norton Healthcare is unlike any health care system in our region. We're innovators and strategic thinkers. We're researchers, leaders and compassionate caregivers. We're a team — no matter your role or location.

Scan the **QR code** to discover a career with no limits. You can also email **recruitment@nortonhealthcare.org** or call **(800) 833-7975** to speak with a recruiter.

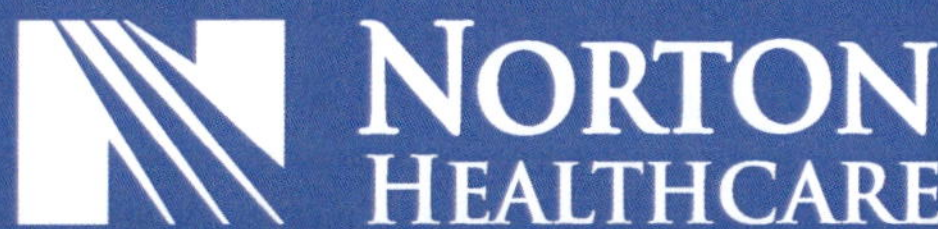

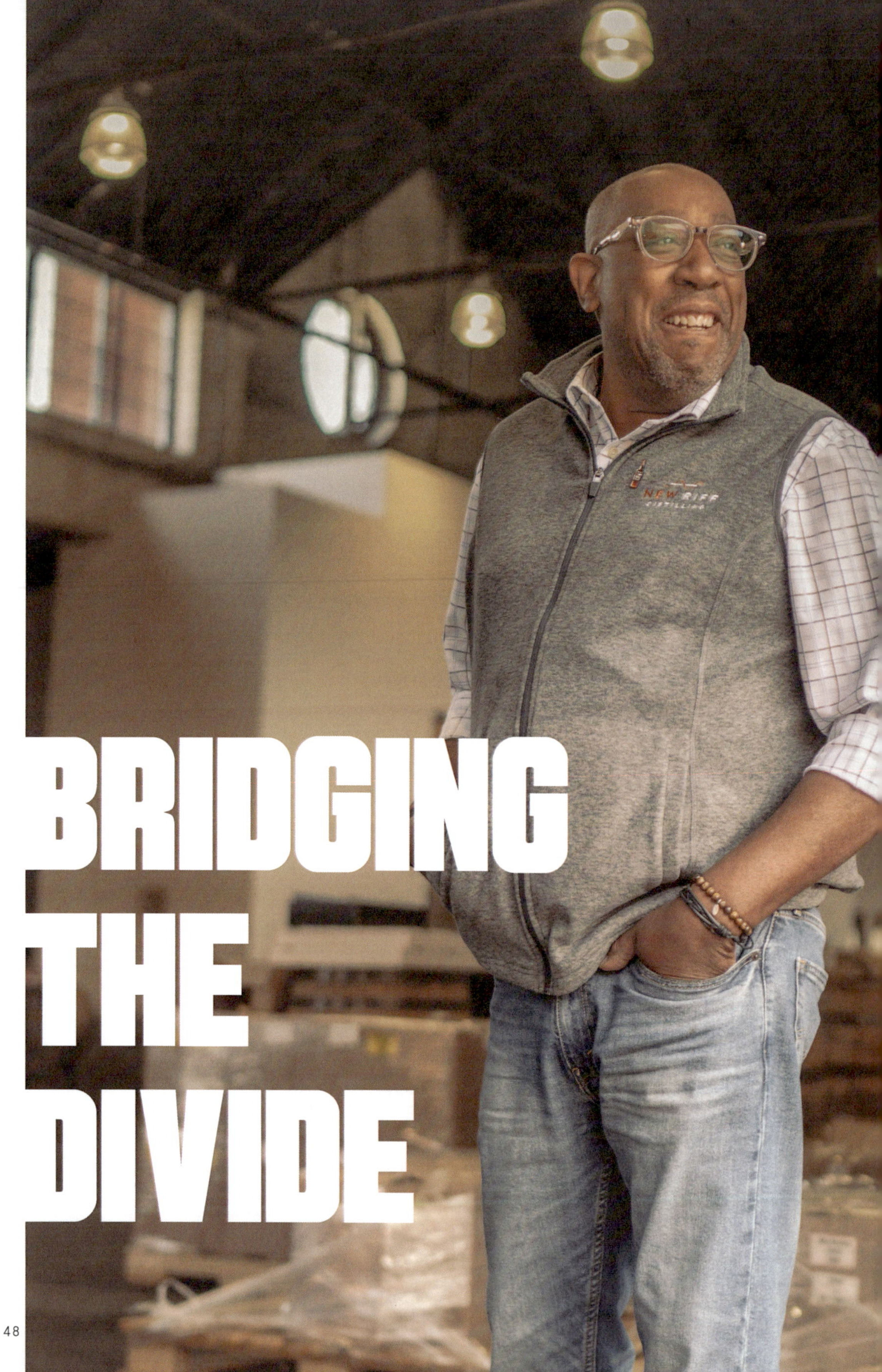

BRIDGING
THE
DIVIDE

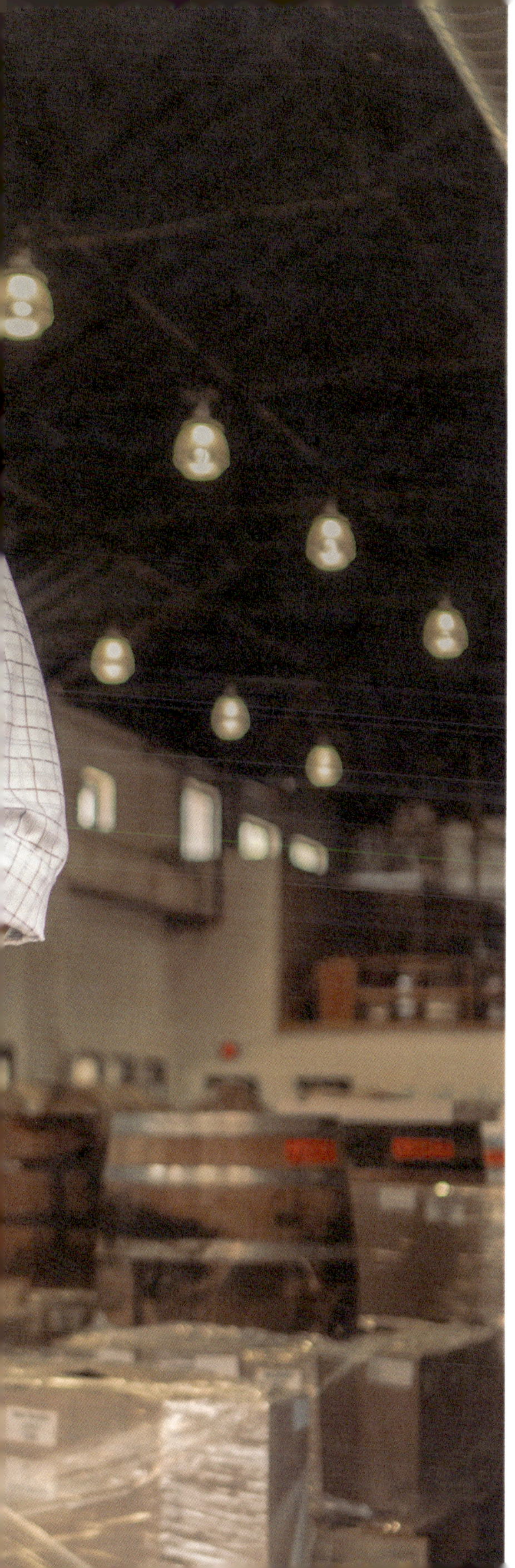

WITH NEW RIFF'S JAY DICKERSON

Kevin Garner
he/him   @gearboxlover45

In a recent study, Coqual.org revealed that approximately 1/3 of Black employees leave corporate America within two years of employment. When I thought about this from the Bourbon industry perspective, I noticed I see very little representation of people of color while on tours of distilleries across the state. This led me to want to know if Black, gay professionals were involved in this industry. Therefore, the opportunity to interview Jay Dickerson piqued my interest to gain a better understanding of how the Bourbon industry works today and it's inclusivity.

Images by Samuel Greenhill   he/him   @abrokenlightbulb

Kevin: What do you do for New Riff Distilling?

Jay: I am a regional sales manager for New Riff Distilling in Newport. I cover six states within my territory, including Ohio. We are known as a "Bottled in Bond" company. In the 1800's, Cincinnati was known as the Bourbon capital of the world. As a result of unsafe practices, the 1897 Bottled in Bond Act was created for consumer safety. I have been with this company for 10 years.

Kevin: What are some trends you see in the Bourbon industry that you feel represent both Black and Queer people? Is "Queer" a term that you're comfortable with?

Jay: I identify as a Black, gay man more so than Queer. However, I'm turning 60 this year and after surviving the 80s and seeing how things have evolved, kids today have done a lot to bring awareness to acceptance for gay people.

Kevin: Being Black and learning acceptance within our world now includes us embracing terms such as Queer, which isn't the worst thing that I've been called in this world.

Jay: I agree.

Kevin: Do you see the Bourbon industry embracing more people of color including people who are gay and/or Queer?

Jay: I think both whiskey and Bourbon are unifiers of people. When you start drinking with someone, you forget about all the other stuff, and remember you're there to enjoy a good drink of choice, you know what I mean?

Kevin: Yes, I do.

Jay: I am not the only LGBTQ+ person working for New Riff. New Riff embraces everyone with their forward thinking. Our company allows for its employees to be themselves. I don't necessarily have to come in as a gay person, but it is OK for me to come as I am and present ideas openly without fear of being ignored or pushed aside. I don't have to hide at all, which is a nice feeling. It only makes the company stronger.

Kevin: What's been the biggest surprise to you working in the industry?

Jay: The ease in which people are accepting Bourbon in their everyday lives. For instance, when I first started people would say that I cannot drink brown liquor.

Kevin: Have you noticed an uptick in representation of Black people within the industry? If so, when? How?

Jay: Yes, Uncle Nearest has done a lot for the industry. The Bourbon industry started with the hard labor of Blacks working and moving barrels. Not only in the Bourbon industry but in the rum industry as well. We are now seeing more Blacks involved with the Bourbon industry. At New Riff we try and be involved with the community as much as possible. We've always been a company that has been known for its inclusivity. I am not the only Black person that works for New Riff. We have several employees who are people of color.

Kevin: Do you believe that race is a factor in the Bourbon industry?

Jay: The Bourbon industry remains a white male cisgendered industry, that's not so necessarily friendly. But I do see it getting better.

Kevin: That's really good to hear! Do you feel the Bourbon industry is making an effort to reach out to the gay/Queer communities?

Jay: Yes, a lot of the bigger companies have the marketing dollars to focus on advertising to these various communities. We are a small company and right now we are expanding our focus as well within those communities.

Kevin: In a perfect world, what would you like to see change in the Bourbon industry?

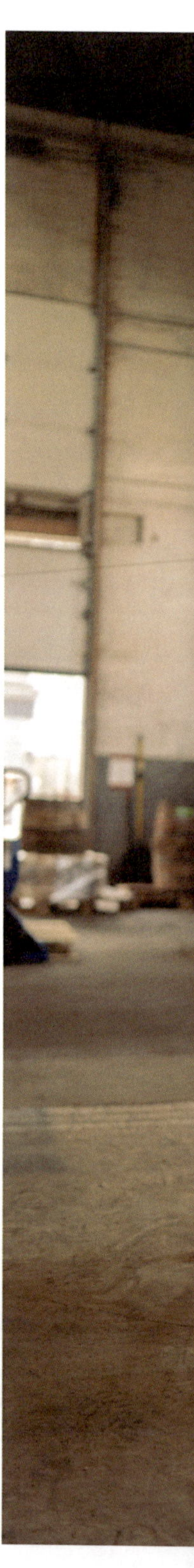

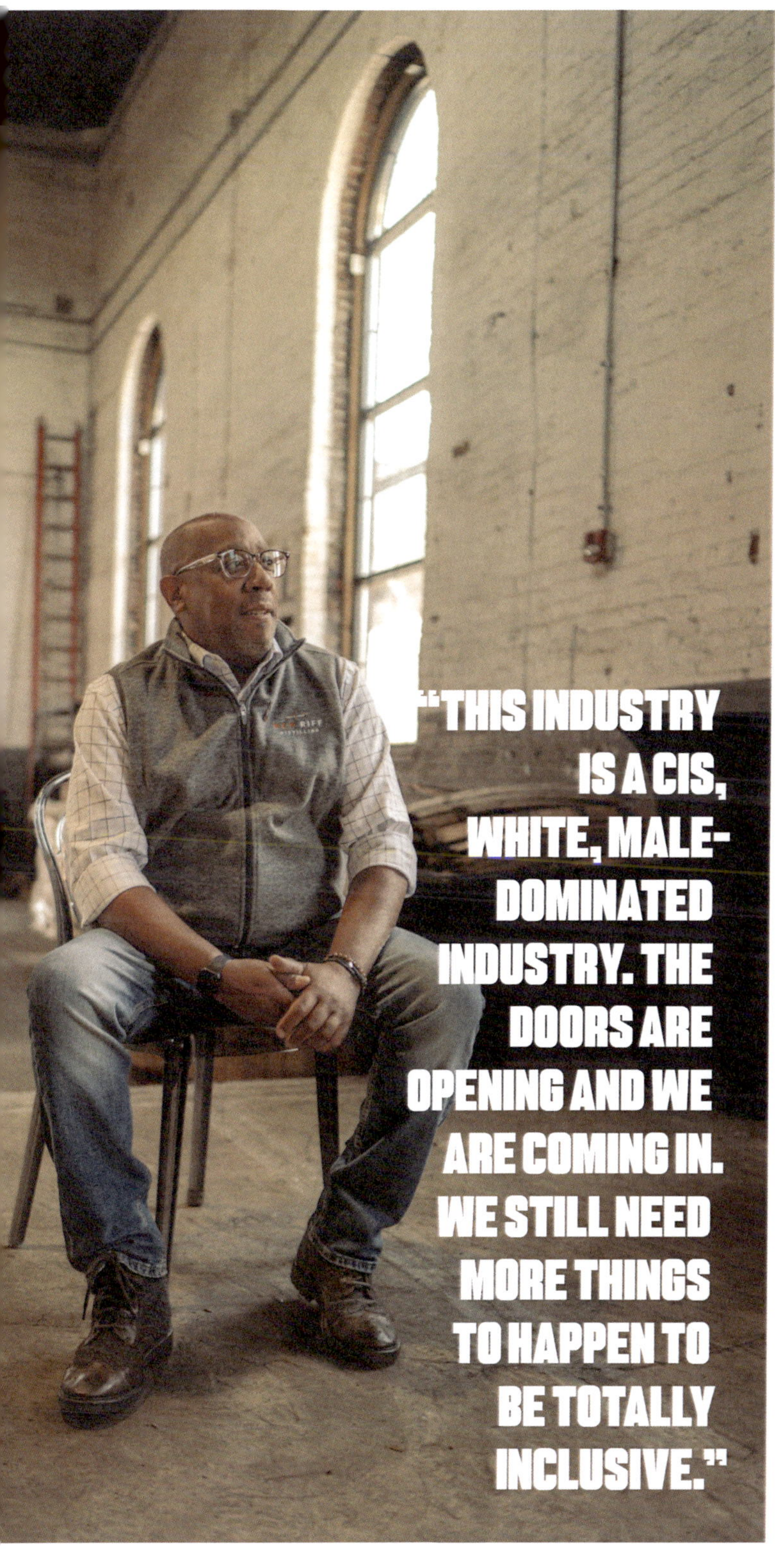

Jay: I don't think of myself as a Queer guy or gay guy per se coming into the Bourbon industry. The Uncle Nearests of the world are moving forward and distilleries are doing the work to bring in more Queer folks and representation. New Riff is a company that the industry is watching and looking at how we are moving within the industry. There is a lot in the business that involves more than making and selling Bourbon. There are lots of opportunities for people of all backgrounds to be involved within the industry.

Kevin: As a Black, gay man, how do you feel your presence at the table impacts the industry? Do you believe more doors can/will be opened as a result?

Jay: This industry is a cis, white, male-dominated industry. The doors are opening and we are coming in. We still need more things to happen to be totally inclusive.

Kevin: Are you walking into rooms and being the only person of color? Possibly the only Queer person?

Jay: There are moments I don't feel welcomed. I really try and not allow this to be my major focus. I have done events and often, I am the only Black guy in the room. Particularly, rural America can be different. But I've found that Bourbon unifies us. Once we start drinking and talking, we learn we are not different.

Thank you, Jay, for taking time to talk to Queer Kentucky. I appreciate you sharing your story and the work you're doing at New Riff.

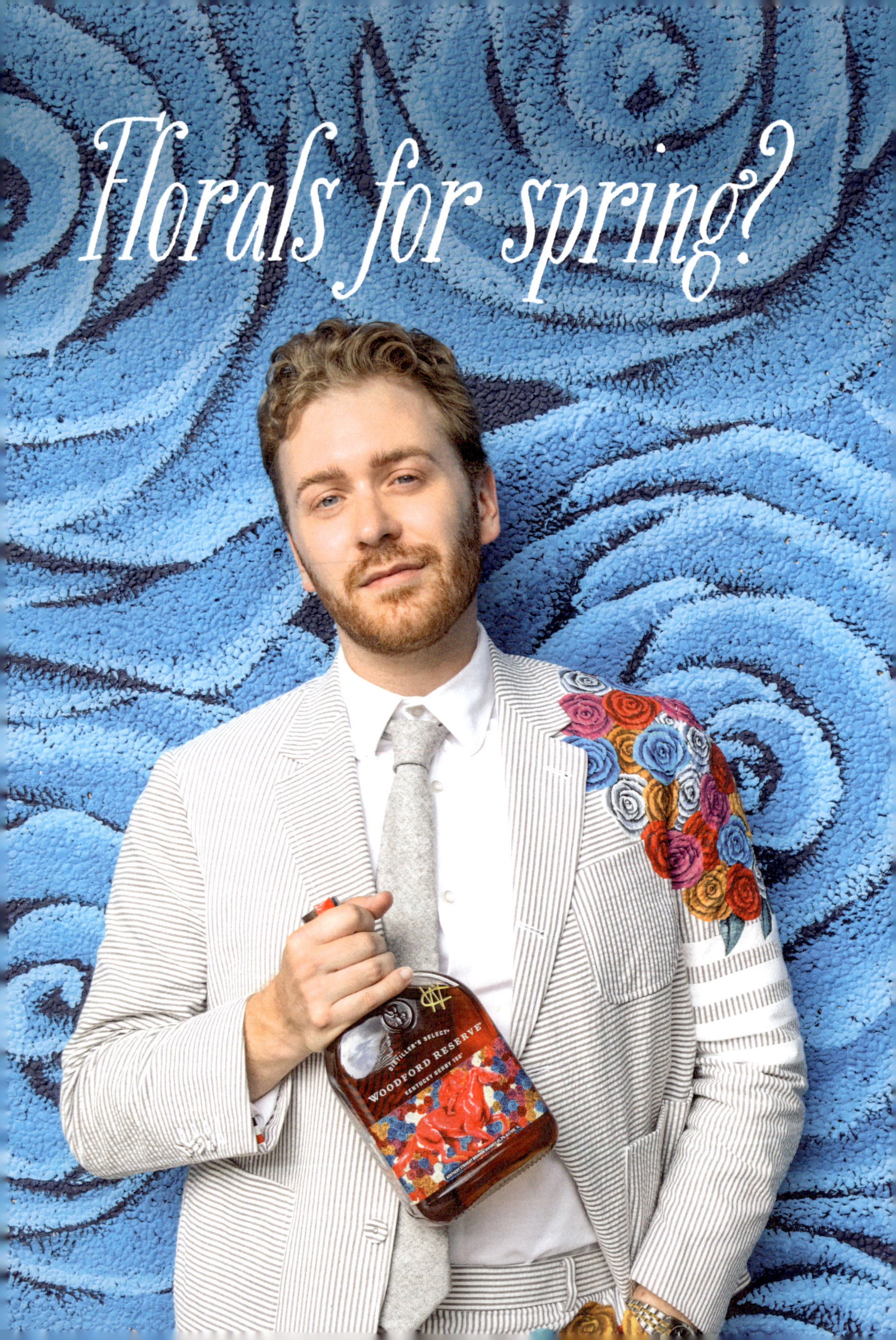
Florals for spring?
DISTILLER'S SELECT
WOODFORD RESERVE
KENTUCKY DERBY 150

Groundbreaking.

Kentucky's newest sweetheart yassifies a Derby tradition

Spencer Jenkins *he/him @spencerjenkss*

Contrary to popular belief, The Kentucky Derby has always been Queer. Big, boisterous hats and flashy fascinators paired with dresses in bright pastels, deep rosy reds and Kentucky blues fill Churchill Downs from the infield to Millionaires row. Let's face it: it's one big drag show.

For the Derby's 150th anniversary, Churchill Downs and Woodford Reserve commissioned openly gay artist, Wylie Caudill, to bring his trademark rosette imagery for the latest design of the famous derby poster and Bourbon bottle. Needless to say, we were absolutely gagged.

Originally from Cynthiana, but now residing in Lexington, Caudill told Queer Kentucky that Woodford Reserve and Churchill Downs had been watching him and his viral social media posts for quite some time before approaching him with the brand deal in January 2023.

Caudill's work went viral in 2021, when over 6 million TikTok users watched Caudill painting a mural of cerulean rosettes with an overlaid audio of The Devil Wears Prada's Mirana Priestly (played by Meryl Streep) delivering a memorable line about a cerulean sweater.

"I think we need a jacket here..."

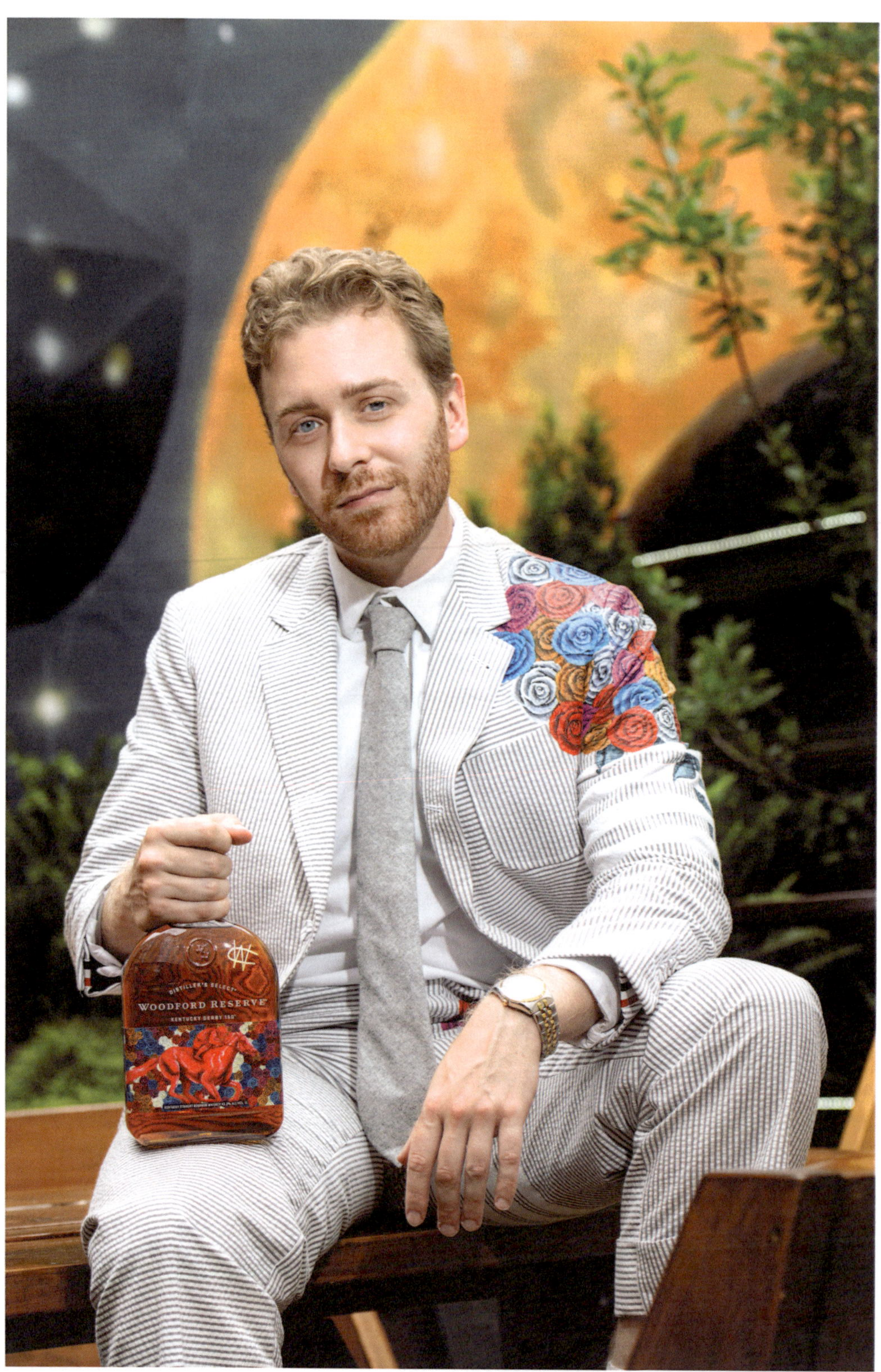

Caudill soon began posting videos of himself painting Woodford Reserve bottles with the famous rosettes. It didn't take long before the bourbon powerhouse brand scouted the painter — the rest is Queerstory.

"For such a momentous occasion for Derby 150, we wanted to feature a Kentucky artist whose work felt different than our past Derby bottles," said Chris Poynter, public relations and partnerships manager for Woodford Reserve and Old Forrester. "We fell in love with Wylie's artwork. And we fell in love with Wylie and his charming and witty personality."

Caudill promoted the partnership beyond his contracted scope of work without hesitation, explaining that he loves showing his work to the world on social media. More specifically, added Caudill, he loves showing Kentucky to the world.

"I don't just 'do' paintings," he stressed. "I do social media. I paint on bottles. I live-paint murals and I was determined to go above and beyond what Churchill Downs and Woodford Reserve have ever had with an artist before."

While the two brands were in love with Caudill's viral work, the process to find the perfect design for Derby 150 didn't come without challenges. Caudill admitted he had little knowledge of Bourbon — or horse racing — which required hours of research to deliver an authentic design that celebrates the Derby's long, rich history.

"I didn't have much of a relationship with Bourbon or the horse industry before this," he said . "I grew up with old retired thoroughbreds in my backyard, but I was never immersed in the culture. They were just these mean old animals in my backyard that I had to feed."

Throughout the whole process, which started in June of 2023, Caudill submitted close to 30 designs to Woodford Reserve and Churchill Downs — many of which were rejected by the brands because they were "too busy" and didn't encompass enough of the style he was known for.

Two weeks before his deadline, he was told that Woodford Reserve and Churchill Downs wouldn't be sharing his design as originally planned. Instead of having a shared design, they would now each have their own.

"Churchill went with the trophy design and Woodford went with the red rose horse," Caudill explained. "I had two weeks to paint them. I am quick, but I'm really really stubborn when I start a project. I can do 16 to 18 hours a day for a week straight and these paintings normally would take three weeks each."

Once the final designs were submitted and approved, Caudill waited over a month in anticipation for the design's release, whch took a toll on his nerves. He vowed not to look at any of the online critics.

When the brands soft-launched the designs on social media, he recalled some of the comments having an effect on him: "Roses aren't blue, what's going on?" one commenter asked.

Then the final designs dropped. As Caudill remembers, the reception took a drastic change for the better — and he took a huge sigh of relief. "I was actually told to read the comments because they were so good," he said with a chuckle.

His hard work for Derby 150 earned Caudill a new kind of brand recognition that's given him a new fan base, and a solid boost in sales for his personal paintings. Within weeks of the release of the designs, his online store sold out.

Oh, and did we mention he's humble too?

"They like me, they really like me," he quipped while doing his best Sally Fields impression.

"To all you other Kentucky Queers out there, you're my heroes, each and every one of you. So you better werk."

WYLIE CAUDILL

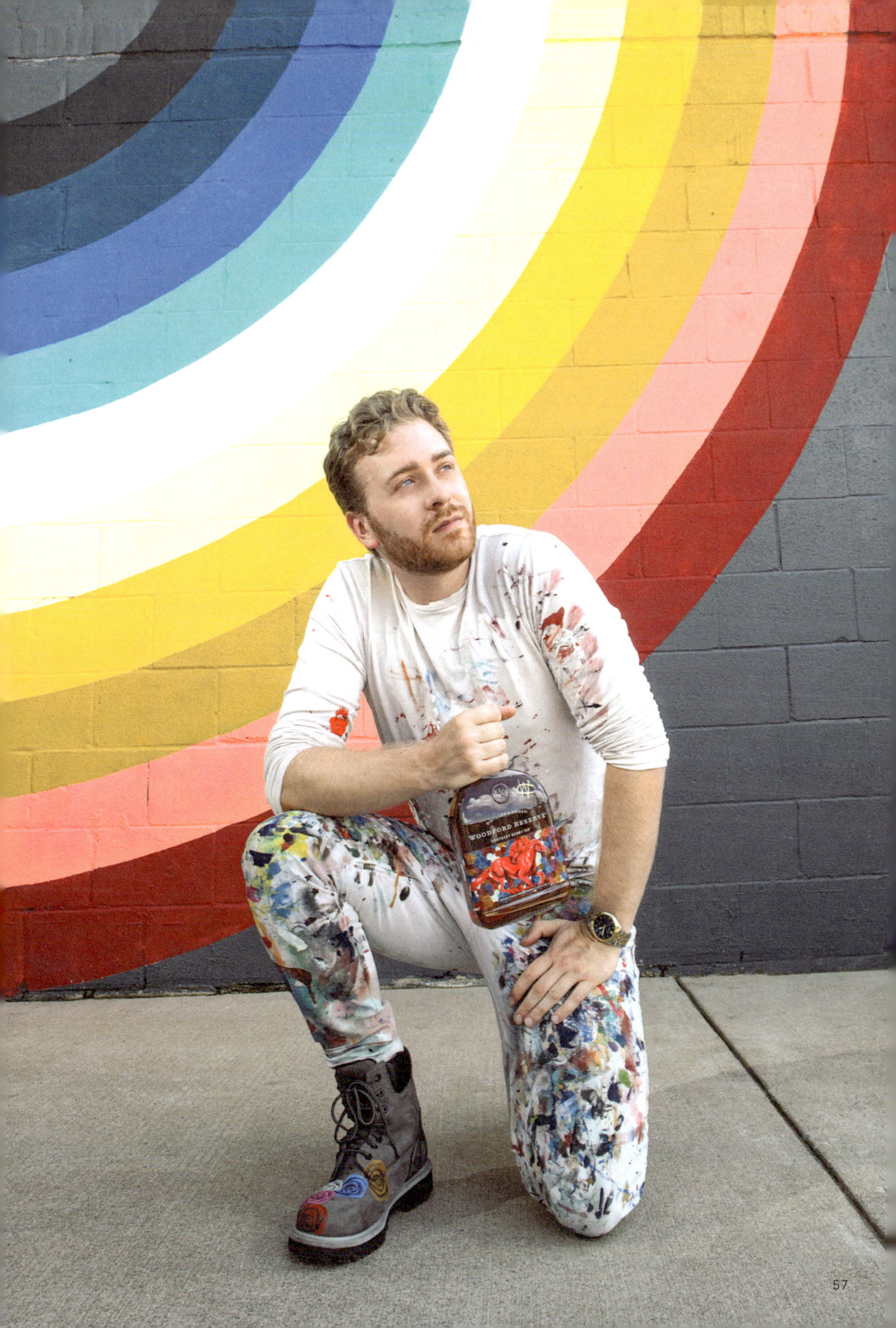

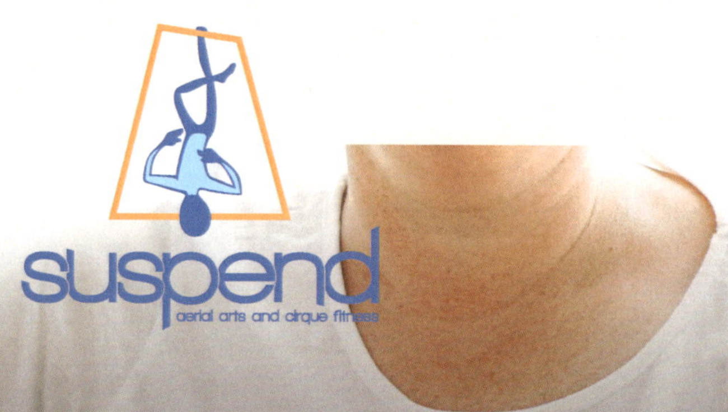

CREATE COMMUNITY AND BECOME CENTERED AT SUSPEND LOUISVILLE.

MINDFUL MOVEMENT IS A BODY INCLUSIVE PRACTICE DESIGNED BY QUEER PEOPLE, FOR QUEER PEOPLE. FREE AND OPEN TO ALL.

SUNDAYS 10 - 10:50 A.M.
721 E WASHINGTON ST., LOUISVILLE, KY 40202

PRIDE IN EVERY POUR

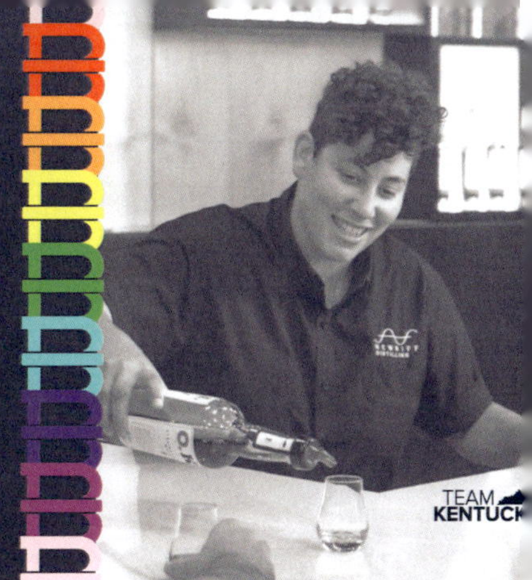

THE **B** LINE.COM

✦ **Business support that meets you where you are!**

Inclusive and training-focused business support

Website Design | **Branding Design**

Graphic Design | **Marketing Support**

Alight Agency is Queer, Appalachian, and Woman Owned, ready to help you run your business with confidence and joy. ✦

AlightAgency.com | @AlightAgency | (859) 351-3542

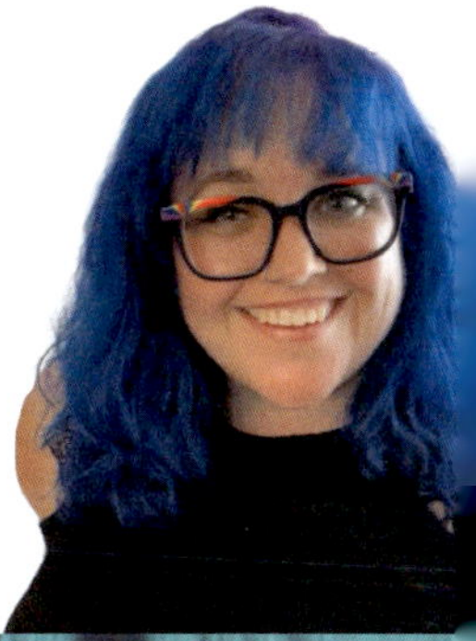

SUMMER'S HOT AND WE'RE DRIPPING WET

SCAN TO COOL OFF

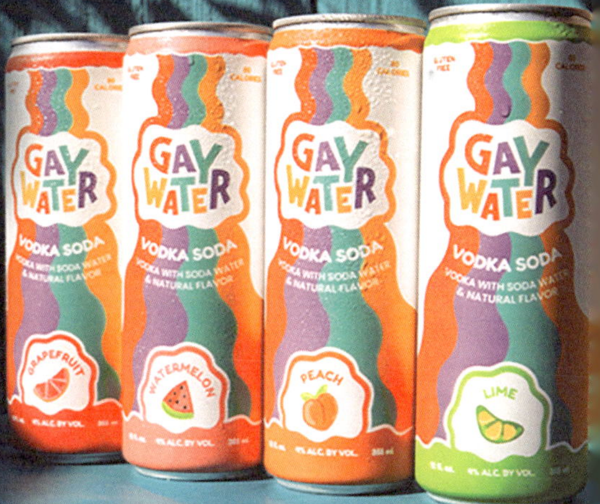

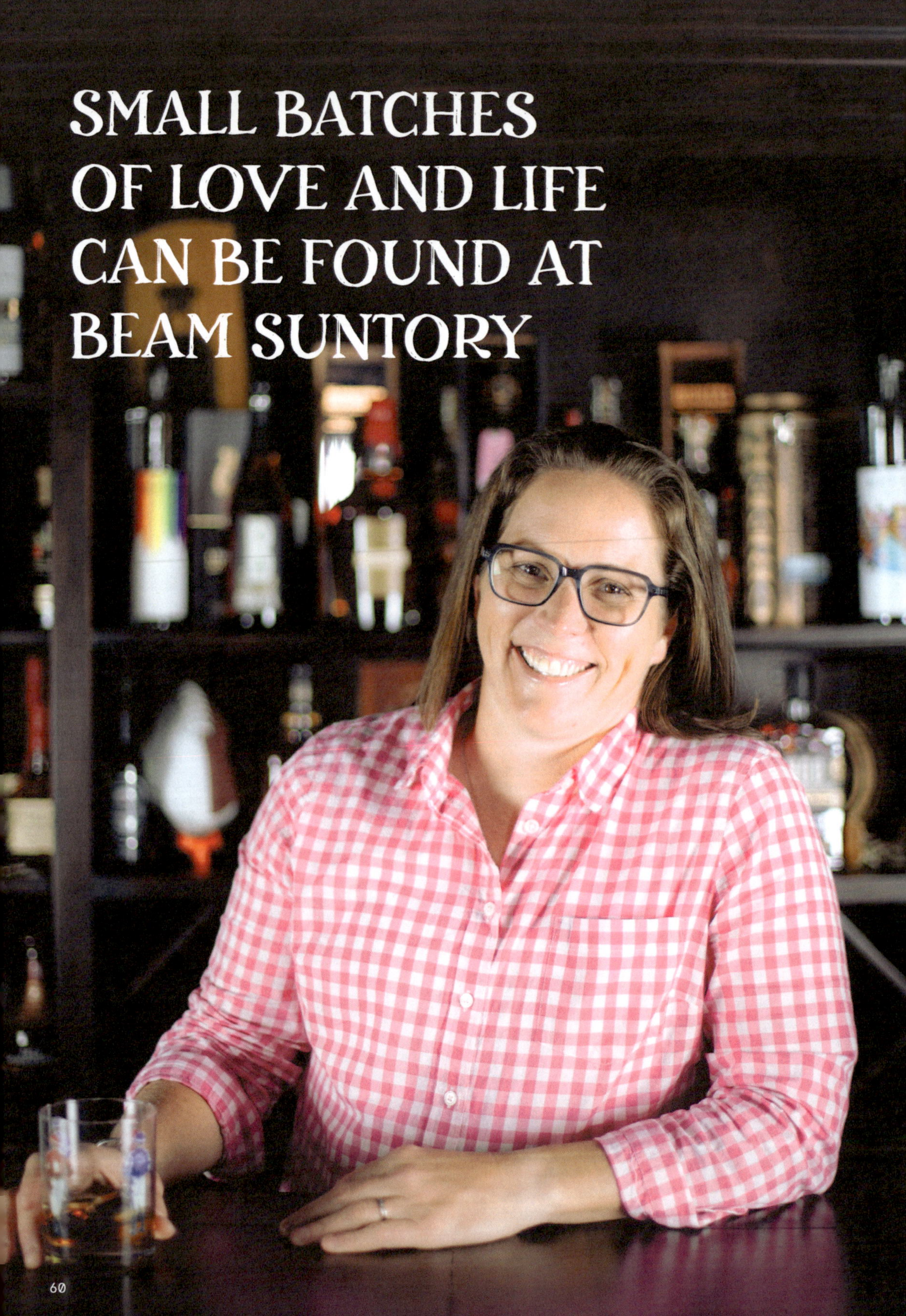

SMALL BATCHES
OF LOVE AND LIFE
CAN BE FOUND AT
BEAM SUNTORY

APRIL ELSTON SHARES HER BREAST CANCER JOURNEY AND THE SUPPORT HER COLLEAGUES SHOWED HER

Nico Lang *he/they* *@Queernewsdaily*

April Elston was at work two years ago when she received an email that would change her life. Test results from an April 2022 biopsy revealed that she had cancer in her right breast, and a series of follow-up calls with her medical team presented a narrow range of treatment options. Elston had three options: have the sole affected breast removed, undergo a double mastectomy, or elect only to have the cancerous mass taken out, meaning that her breasts would remain otherwise intact. During these conversations, her mind was flooded with questions. She wondered: What if it's in my lymph nodes? What if they're not able to treat it? What is it going to do to me? What is it going to do to my family?

A part of her, she says, was preparing to die.

For her entire life, Elston has been someone with a logical, scientific mind. As the senior manager for the whiskey research and innovation team at Beam Suntory, the world's third-largest producer of alcoholic beverages, she likes to have all the facts before she moves ahead: whether that's on a new work project or in raising the two children she shares with her wife. But now that she was barrelling forward into the unknown, the uncertainties of what she was experiencing utterly terrified her.

"I didn't want to make the wrong decision," she says. "Literally, my life was on the line."

Ultimately, Elston opted to have a double mastectomy, which took place exactly 40 days after her initial diagnosis. Because her lymph nodes tested negative for cancer, she did not have to undergo chemotherapy treatment, which can be physically grueling.

The most difficult part of adjusting to life after her surgery, Elston says, was navigating the myriad (and ongoing) changes in her body. She used to run 25 miles a week, including a half marathon each weekend. But during her convalescence, Elston says it was "humbling" to need her wife's help to wash herself or even be able to climb into the shower. It took eight weeks before she went in for chest reconstruction surgery, during which time she had a chest expander to help make room for the implants.

"If you use expanders, they essentially will stitch onto your chest these metal expanders and then they slowly inflate them," she explains. "It stretches your skin. I constantly felt it, and I couldn't get back to myself. My wife and I called them waves: We'd just have to take on one wave at a time, whether it was doctor's appointments, the cancer, or surgeries. Whatever life offered to us, we just took it one step at a time."

Even two years later, Elston acknowledges that some facets of her existence are fundamentally different, and they may never go back to the way they were before. These days, Elston finds shopping for bathing suits to be a miserable experience, and she can no longer wear a typical, off-the-rack bra due to her implants, which her plastic surgeon compared to "two hamburgers." ("They don't have the mountaintops," he had advised her.)

She rarely ever went to the doctor prior to her diagnosis—aside from her annual physical exam—but she now has to make regular appointments to get infusions of calcium in her bones. Last year, she underwent a full hysterectomy to lessen the chances of breast cancer recurrence.

But despite her fears about what cancer would take from her, Elston says that, for the most part, her life today feels profoundly normal. She credits that, in no small way, to her employer. When she was finally able to return to work, Elston says that she was heartened that none of the other members of her team treated her with "kid gloves." "It made me feel like I was my old self, like I wasn't being treated any differently from before I had cancer," she recalls. "I wanted to make sure that I could get back to it, and it was about proving to myself that I could."

Although she didn't want to be coddled at a job where she had worked for eight years, Elston notes that her fellow coworkers did go out of their way to show her that she was loved and supported: buying her gift cards, offering to pay for meals, and recommending books to read on cancer recovery. The master distiller at Beam Suntory's Louisville office, Freddie Noe, even created a special edition of his whiskey brand, Little Book, to raise money for breast cancer treatment and prevention.

Elston was heartened to see her coworkers unanimously have her back—because when she first moved to Kentucky to work for Beam Suntory now 10 years ago, Elston admits that she wasn't sure what to expect.

While she says that her mother was a "huge Jim Beam drinker," referencing the company's flagship brand, Elston hadn't yet developed the taste for Bourbon. She has since come to appreciate the liquor's richness, complexity, and its wide variety of flavors, Elston says. Whereas she describes the vodka as uniformly "colorless and odorless," she enjoys the creativity of Bourbon, searching for the notes of vanilla or caramel hidden deep within the batch.

And as an out Queer woman, Elston wasn't sure how she fit in with that world. She had never even visited Kentucky prior to the move and she was concerned that she wouldn't be accepted; having her work family there to help find her new normal was just one more indication of how unfounded those old apprehensions were.

> Since they were very little, Elston says that she has regularly brought her children with her to the distillery to show them "what Mommy does" for a living, and she has never taken for granted–even for a moment–that she feels comfortable enough to do that.

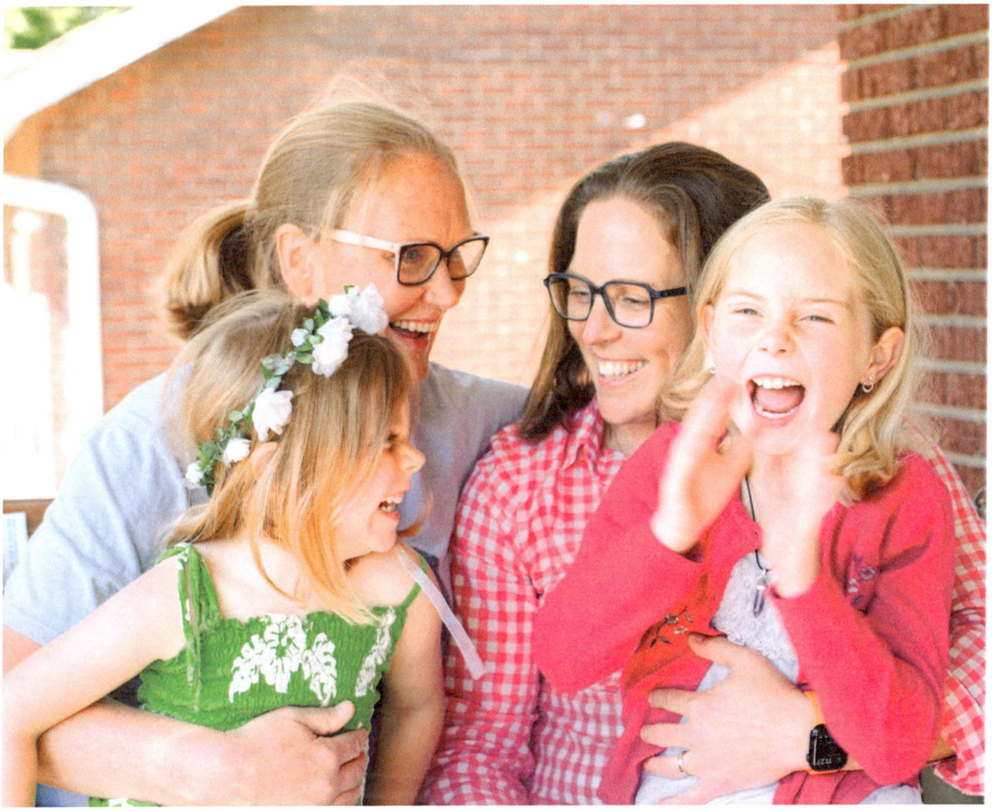

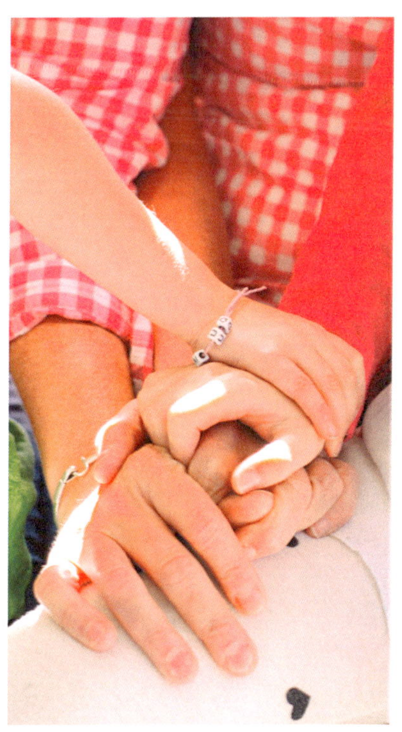

"I didn't know what I was going to walk into, but I came in and said, 'This is me,'" she says. "I was given some advice back in college: 'If you don't make a big deal about things, other people don't make a big deal about things.'

"I love my life, and being gay doesn't hinder me. It doesn't negate anything that I bring to the table here at work. It's just another piece of who I am."

"WE CAN'T FORGET ABOUT THE PEOPLE OF WHITESBURG"

THE SPIRIT, FIGHT, AND RESILIENCE OF MICHELE HOBBS

Missy Spears

she/they   *@missy.spears*

Nothing that I describe to you, from her nonstop energy to her multiple successful businesses to the Bourbon that we initially intended to speak about, sums Michele Hobbs up better than her insistence on turning all conversations to the people of Whitesburg, Kentucky.

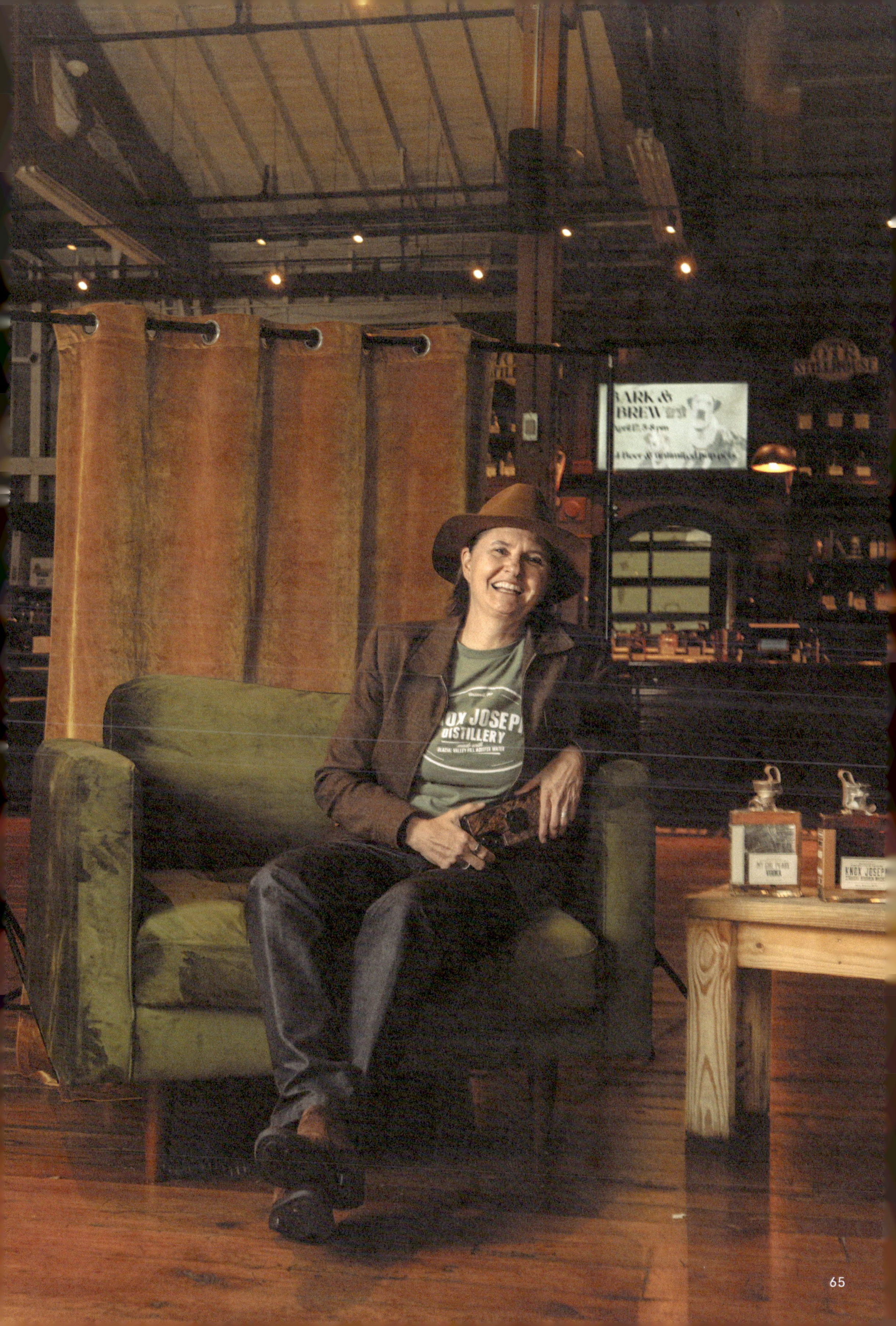

So let's start with Whitesburg. Located in Letcher County and right on the Kentucky/ Virginia border, Whitesburg is the home of 2,321 working-class and working-poor Kentuckians. It's the place where Hobbs spent a large part of her childhood running around outdoors, fishing, and learning what community is all about. And if you look at Hobbs' life now, it's still filled with a lot of running around outdoors, fishing, and showing others what community is about.

Now living in Cincinnati, Hobbs returns to Whitesburg regularly to take her young kids fishing in the same waters that she grew up in. After the 2022 flooding that decimated parts of Whitesburg, it's a place that she's returned to time and time again with food, supplies, and an army of community behind her.

When news of the flooding broke, Hobbs didn't ask what she could do. She just did it. "The flood happened overnight July 27. In Letcher County, where I call home, my family was inline with a direct hit in the floods. We turned to friends, businesses and strangers to bring attention and help to the people of Letcher County. Although the path of destruction ran from before Jackson and through Whitesburg, we chose to focus on Letcher County, specifically, Isom and Blackey. This is where I have family, and had people I could trust, whom I

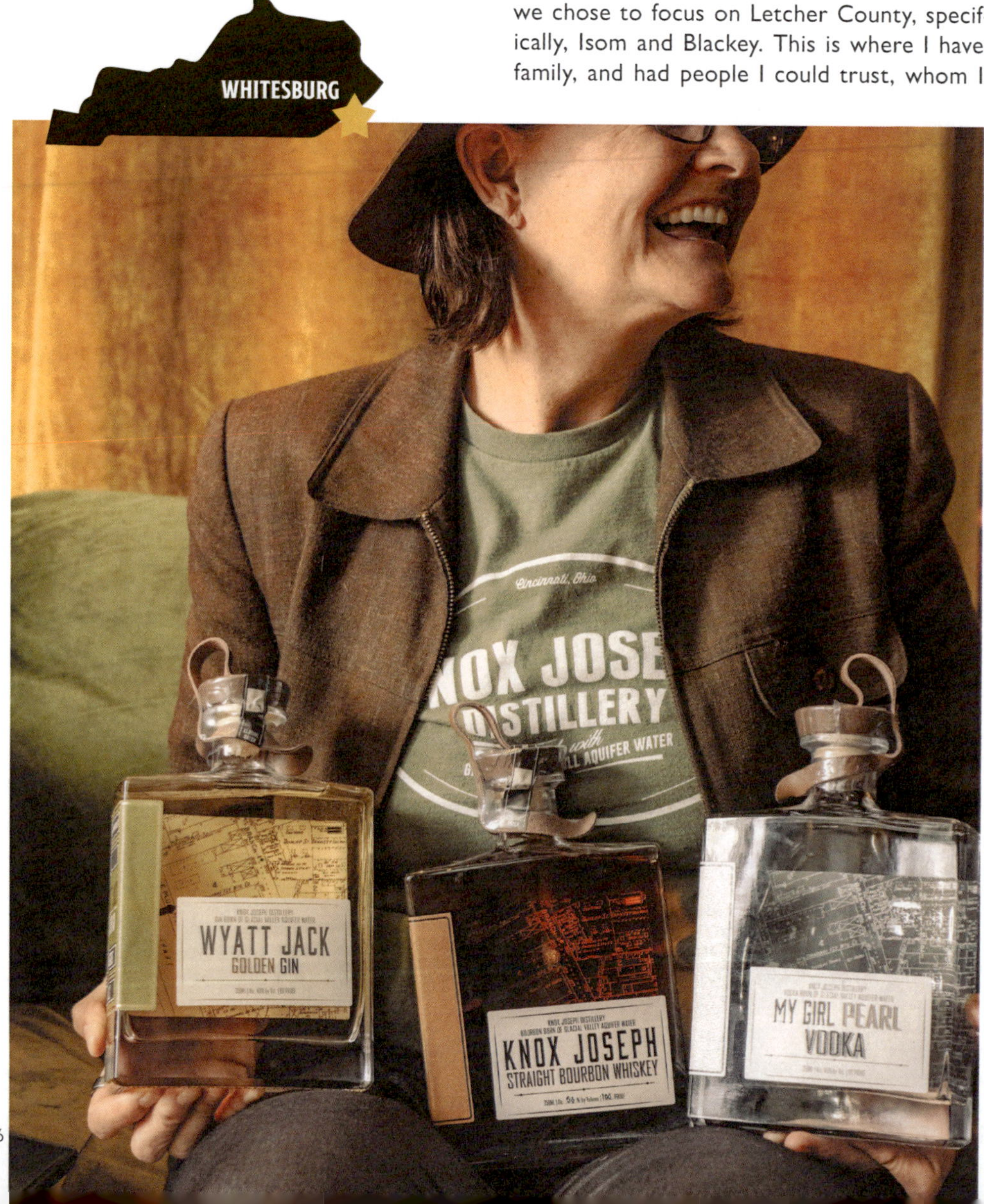

could work directly with, therefore getting aid in immediately."

Using her own network and resources to provide immediate aid, Hobbs started fundraising for the region, ultimately raising over $5,500 in just five days. Money that funded essentials, including the purchase of 60 charcoal grills complete with charcoal for each grill, as well as a truck that helped haul it all to a temporary warehouse. Hobbs worked with former Kentucky Democratic House Minority Whip Rachel Roberts to get power to that building, a building that is still being used to this day.

During those first few days, Hobbs' friend Suzy DeYoung, founder of La Soupe, a Cincinnati-based nonprofit dedicated to fighting food insecurity and waste, had been in contact with her friends at the World Central Kitchen. In only three days, they were set up in the IGA parking lot in Isom, cooking meals for thousands each day and teaching others in the community how to replicate their efforts. Hobbs recalls, "LaSoupe began making multiple trips a week to Letcher County with hundreds of meals, donating to pantries, schools and families. Suzy built a coalition of friends to help, and soon she was teaching the folks at the CANE Kitchen in Whitesburg how to feed hundreds of people out of the little volunteer kitchen… They were feeding 2000 people 3 meals a day!"

With their needs outgrowing the 60 grills they brought down, Hobbs knew they needed to work fast to scale their grassroots operation. A few days later, 504 more grills, a semi-truck of charcoal, and pallets of cleaning supplies came pouring in thanks to partnerships with regional corporations. The months that followed included rebuilding efforts within the community, as well as additional fundraising events, including an all day festival called "Hope for the Hills" that raised $22,000 for the area and was held at Hobbs' very own OTR Stillhouse at Knox Joseph Distillery.

The OTR Stillhouse, located in the Over-the-Rhine neighborhood of Cincinnati, was opened to the public in 2021 and serves as the home of Knox Joseph Distillery, the creator of award-winning Bourbon, blended whiskies, and gins. When Hobbs decided to purchase the giant building at 2017 Branch Street, and the previous home of the Standard Ice Manufacturing Company, it was intended to be a warehouse for her quickly scaling pet food brand Pet Wants. A lifelong hustler, entrepreneur, and expert of identifying industry needs, Pet Wants launched as pet food store catering to the growing demand for high-quality, allergy-friendly pet food. From its humble beginnings tabling at events and growing to a single brick and mortar within Cincinnati's legendary Finley Market, Pet Wants exploded into a nationally known brand with over a hundred franchises, making Hobbs one of the few LGBTQ+ and female entrepreneurs receiving national attention for her work.

Never one to shy away from identifying an opportunity, those plans changed when Hobbs discovered the aquifer of fresh, clean water that ran below the building, a discovery that caused her to pivot toward her lifelong dream of owning a Bourbon distillery. Almost a decade later, Hobbs now runs one of the few LGBTQ+ and female-owned distilleries in the country: A sprawling venue where her commitment to family and community can take on a life of its own. Supported by her wife Amanda, she has created a space designed to serve as a community hub, fueled by a desire to create an environment so welcoming and inclusive that it has the power to pull people out of their caves and into community. Fundraisers, concerts, and Pride markets happen regularly here, as do special one-time events like a screening of the Indigo Girls documentary and a private gathering of local leaders, bartenders, and business owners focused on creating an emergency response system for the LGBTQ+ community.

Living in a world still finding its footing since the height of the pandemic, Hobbs' story is a reminder of the power of human connection, the importance of community engagement, and the resilience of the entrepreneurial spirit. And the eternal truth that Kentucky stays with you forever.

No Regrets

KRISTIN SMITH'S JOURNEY FROM WILLIAMSBURG
TO WANDERLUST TO HOME IN WRIGLEY'S TAPROOM

Austyn Gaffney
she/her   @austyngaffney

LEE INITIATIVE LUNCH BREAK

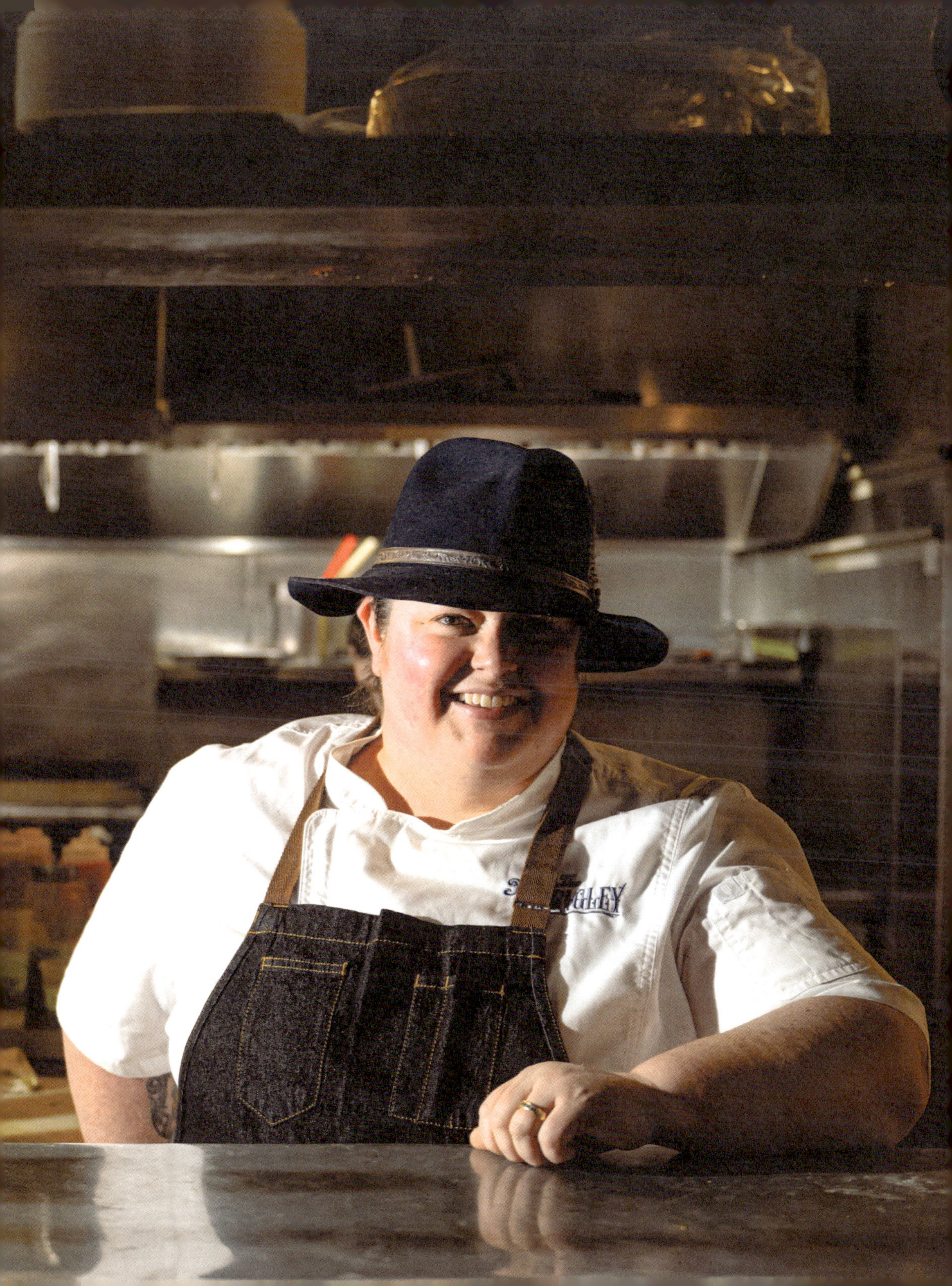

Along Main Street in downtown Corbin, across the street from White Rabbit Records and next to the pinball museum, Wrigley's Taproom & Eatery celebrated its ninth birthday earlier this year. That party was the culmination of star chef Kristin Smith's return to Eastern Kentucky more than 15 years ago.

The move home for Smith (she/they) wasn't part of their plan: Smith was at seminary school in San Francisco back in 2008 when she got a call from her grandfather.

"I never thought I would go home. Because I was Appalachian, and if you want to make something of yourself, you leave. There was nothing here for us at the time that I was growing up. That was the narrative we all told ourselves," said Smith from the upstairs office of her restaurant. But their grandfather had called. He told Smith he had stomach cancer, and he needed someone to take over the farm. They decided to try it for five years. If she ended up miserable, at least she'd given it a good go.

"There's this innate part of me that I cannot live with any regret; it's kind of how I've always made decisions," Smith told me. "I didn't want this to feel like this will be a core regret in my life."

When they got there, the third of an acre garden had become a bit of a dump. A trio of parked cars rusted on top of it. She was tilling silverware and old rugs out of the soil. She met a group of local female farmers through the county extension agency, and together they started a farmer's market. One of the local food boosters was a woman named Melissa, who eventually became Smith's wife.

Smith sold beef cattle and hogs, turning the product into popular tacos and sandwiches every weekend for customers. Eventually, two other food vendors approached her and asked her to go in on a restaurant with them. When she visited the building, they'd pulled back the sheet rock that hid an old Wrigley's Spearmint sign, the eccentric marketing campaign from the chewing gum company founded in 1891. William Wrigley Jr., the company's founder, had distributed promotional booklets that told the story of the Spearmen — small, elfin characters who wore monochromatic clothes and triangular hats. In Wrigley's taproom, the titular character dons an orange cloke and cap, pointing towards a pack of gum near the front window.

"I walked in and I thought, oh, this is something special," said Smith. It was bare bones, but she couldn't say no. The historic sign, the high ceilings, the big open space for a long community table — it all felt right to her. She knew if she drove by later and saw someone else in charge, she'd regret it, and she couldn't live with regrets.

Today, she sees the space as a "table for all people." A sign above the door says the Wrigley Taproom & Eatery "strives to CARE for and NURTURE our community in mind, body and spirit, one INSPIRED plate at a time."

"I want to have a place of dialogue because I think that's the only way we're going to go forward," said Smith. "And it happens on a daily basis. We have totally different spectrums of people sitting right next to each other."

But it took a while for Smith to get to a place where she too could embody her full spectrum. When they left home initially for college, they didn't go far, just across the state border to a small Christian university in East Tennessee. There, they majored in religious studies and after graduation, she moved to China for a three-year stint as a missionary under the Southern Baptist International Mission Board.

"Joining up as a missionary was probably part of me trying to save myself," Smith reflected. She was eventually kicked out of the program because she confessed to having fallen in love with a fellow female-identifying missionary. The experience nearly destroyed her. She moved out to San Francisco for seminary school, but she was conflicted about what came next. "I think I had more questions than I had answers," she said.

The experience scarred her, and after she moved home, she was quiet about her relationship with Melissa. If they wanted to go on public dates, they'd head to bigger cities. In 2021, about six years after opening her restaurant, Smith put up a rainbow flag for the first time behind the bar during Pride month.

"I don't know if I necessarily started this business out thinking we'd be a safety beacon," said Smith. "But it became more and more clear to me, when my wife and I were going to Lexington or Knoxville or Louisville just to be on dates, that it was something I could foster in my own restaurant. If we need that, there might be a lot of others who might not have the access or ability to leave. So that became a lot more intentional."

Still, she was nervous, and on July 1, 2021, she took the flag down and breathed a sigh of relief, thinking okay, they made it through. The next summer, she hung the Pride flag again and planned to remove it again, but her staff begged her to keep it up. She said part of her initial hesitation was mental, but she's also lost friendships and experienced family strain due to her sexuality and her same-sex marriage.

But then, in 2023, legislation started changing, removing rights for transgender people in the LGBTQ+ community.

"It scared me," said Smith. "I thought we were going backwards instead of forwards."

For years, the restaurant had two single-use gender-neutral bathrooms, but Smith wanted to do more to make sure trans and nonbinary people knew they were welcome. So she changed the flag again, putting up an all-inclusive Rainbow flag that highlighted equality for the trans community and BIPOC folks that took up the brick wall behind the bar year-round.

"If I go down because I welcome trans men and women, I'm okay with it. I've also been here nine years, and I think I've proven a lot for myself and our community," said Smith. "But the fear is there, everyday, that it could happen."

Some days, she's surprised the doors to Wrigley's are still open, but she says she owes the success to her incredible staff, who she calls "salt of the earth people" and "the community that values us enough and our work and who we are that has kept us here."

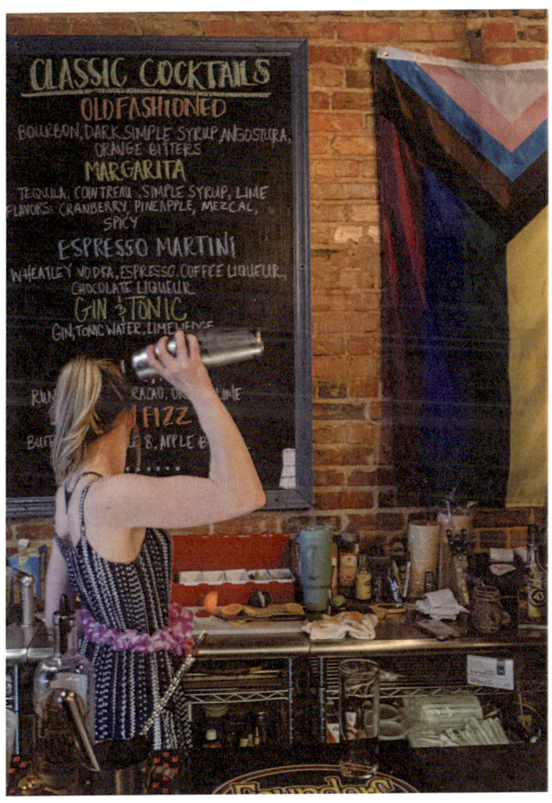

Wrigley's is known not only for its inventive dishes — when we visited, they were celebrating Tiki Week over Corbin's spring break, allowing parents who couldn't travel to still experience an escape with rum-themed cocktails and mahi mahi on the menu — but also for its hospitality, for its community table, and for its tendency to lean into difficult conversations instead of gloss over them. Smith, a chatty, engaged listener, quick to laugh and grin, is perhaps the perfect host to bring that community to Corbin.

Across the bar from the rainbow flag, an American flag hangs above the gender-neutral bathrooms. Here, framing the fluorescent EXIT sign, Smith painted a phrase that perhaps embodies her take on a complex life: "Every EXIT is an entrance somewhere."

"THE KENTUCKY GENT" SERVES THE BLUEGRASS & BOURBON WITH SPIRITED LOVE

Tom Lally *he/him* *@tomlallyky*

Josh Johnson is a Kentucky gentleman. That's how he put it to fashion industry leaders from New York to Los Angeles while working as a clothing buyer more than a decade ago. Folks followed the phrase with confused looks and questioning glances at Johnson's long hair and tattooed skin. "You're not really what we expected someone from Kentucky to look like," they'd say.

While fried chicken, barley and Bourbon have space in his heart, Johnson represents Kentucky in a way only he can, by being himself. To him, that's what a Kentucky Gentleman is.

"People assume something about someone based on locality or sexual orientation or identity and pigeonhole people into a monolith," he said.

Johnson, better known for his digital alter ego "The Kentucky Gent," runs a men's life and style blog by the same name. He acts as a gateway to the south, just like his hometown of Louisville. It also doesn't hurt to remind the world that Southern boys have taste.

Like most Kentuckians, Johnson has a thing or two to say about Bourbon. "It's legacy and connection, something to be proud of," Johnson said. He went on to describe the Bourbon renaissance we're seeing in the Commonwealth; renewed interest in a classic spirit driving the state's economic development while bolstering tourism in towns big and small. He said, "I think the only way to improve that would be to show more inclusivity and more people that drink Bourbon versus it just being kind of pigeonholed into, 'It's a man's drink.'"

Let's be clear, Bourbon is not just a man's drink. It's Kentucky's spirit, it belongs to all of us and none of us. Its unique and celebrated flavor is the product of local ingredients and time spent aging in the bluegrass.

Like Kentucky Bourbon, Johnson's lived experience as a gay man blends with Southern style and culture to create the perfect cocktail of a blog. Queer people aren't new to Kentucky, but their representation is, and Johnson takes that to heart when sharing his stories.

"That was never really shown for me," he recalled, describing his religious upbringing in Southern Indiana. Christian Satellite TV, a service that is still around today, was Johnson's main source of media as a child, reaffirming the lessons he learned from his parents. The religious lessons he learned at home and through media only supplemented the teaching of his family church.

Those teachings came to a head when Johnson's family discovered he was gay. At the age of fourteen, an online love interest outed him to his preacher. His life, both online and at home, would never be the same.

In time, he moved to Kentucky for the space he needed to grow. Like barley and bluegrass in the summer sun, he received the nurture and care he needed from his community and from himself. Now, he shares his experience with the world, one post at a time.

In the same way he hopes to introduce the world to Southern culture, he hopes to introduce young Queer people to a new world of opportunities. Through his own story, he shows youth that it's possible to hold space in their communities without being subjugated to stereotypical identities and roles.

In a December 2014 blog post titled "Coming Out," Johnson wrote, "It's my wish that as time goes on I can be a positive role model for young people, especially young gay men and

that this site will serve as inspiration for them. A source of inspiration that shows that they can be anything that they put their mind to, be whomever they wish to be, and be bigger than any labels placed on them by others."

In the time since that post, Johnson has led by example, not just for Kentucky, but also for towns big and small across the country. From South Carolina to Texas and Illinois, he tells stories of exciting attractions and refreshing oases with a sense of charred charm that only Kentucky's Bourbon and gentleman can offer.

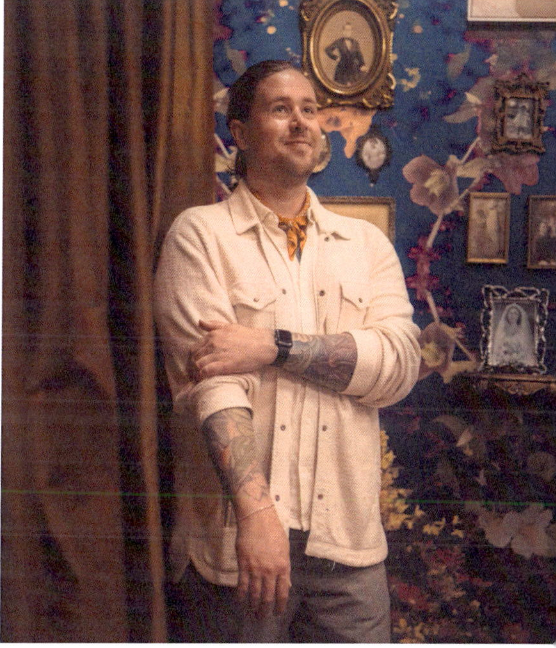

So, who is the Kentucky Gentleman? He's a son working to build a relationship with his family while maintaining healthy boundaries. He's a gay man who watches Star Wars, plays video games, and drinks Old Fashions in his Germantown home. He's a marketing professional who spends his days empowering communities across America to reach new audiences and support LGBTQ+ tourism.

When you think of the Commonwealth, leave the stereotypes and fried chicken behind and remember, Kentucky - and its gentlemen - have more to offer.

... Okay, maybe remember the fried chicken too.

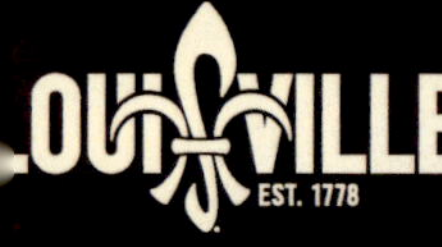

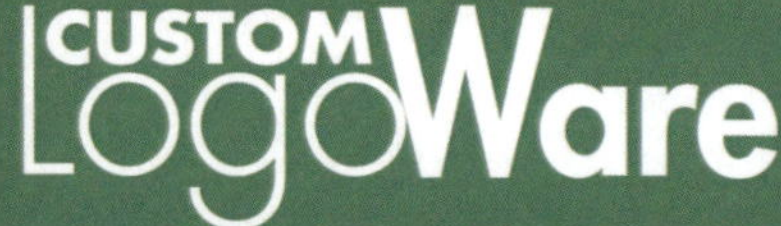

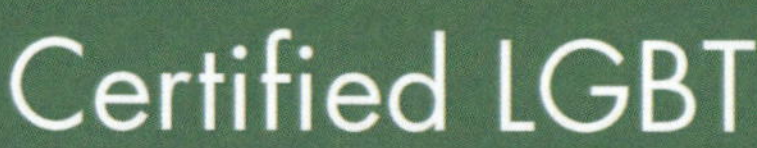

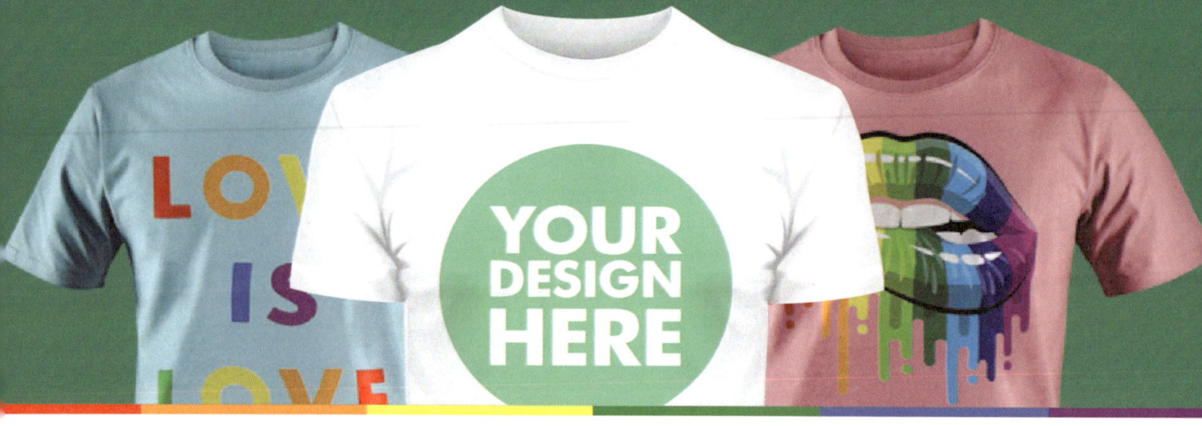

Custom Apparel & Branded Promotional Items

www.CustomLogoWare.com

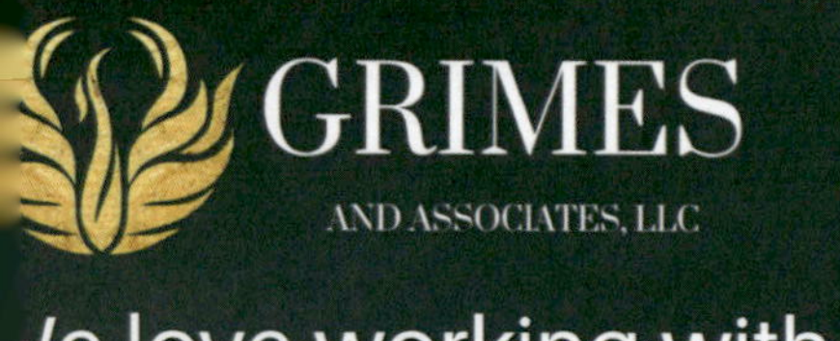

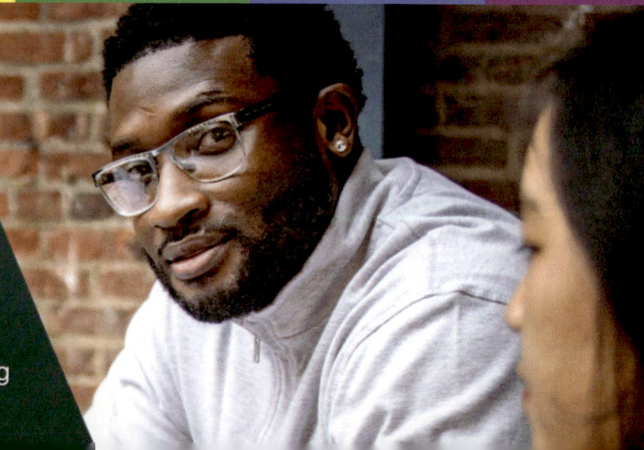